The Crowing
of the Roosters

Fransje van Riel

with

Nomfusi Vinah Yekani

For Joyce,
Best Wishes,
Fransje

First published in 2004 in Southern Africa by
David Philip Publishers, an imprint of New Africa Books (Pty) Ltd,
99 Garfield Road, Claremont 7700, South Africa

www.newafricabooks.co.za

© text Fransje van Riel and Nomfusi Vinah Yekani 2004
© published text New Africa Books 2004

ISBN 0-86486-654-2

Edited by Jennifer Stastny
Proofread by Kathy Sutton
Cover design by Toby Newsome
Design and typesetting by Charlene Bate
Map by André Plant
Printed and bound by MSP Print

Some names have been changed to protect the identities of family
members and those who prefer not to be named.

Quote on page 93 from *The Long Journey of Poppie Nongena* by Elsa Joubert.
Published by Jonathan Ball Publishers, Johannesburg and Cape Town.

Acknowledgements

Thank you, Nomfusi Vinah Yekani, for sharing with me, and the world, your wonderful stories and inspirational memories. You are truly an exceptional person!

I'd like to thank my family – Jan, Ton, Daisy and Anne van Riel – for their support and love; and thanks Pap for being the email link between Vinah and myself.

Thank you Gareth Patterson for your love, patience and companionship.

I would also like to thank my extended family, Jan and Annemarie van Riel, and the following people whose belief, input and encouragement have been of such great importance in the writing this book: Tanja Hendriks, Ingrid Meurs, and the rest of the Arena team in The Netherlands for their enthusiasm and unfailing belief in the story; and, in Cape Town, Brian Wafawarowa, Jeanne Hromnik, my fabulous editor Jen Stastny and everyone else at New Africa Books. I would further like to thank my good friend Liezel Mortimer and Euginia Mcinga-Dladla at the Knysna Library for their assistance with this book as well as David Tyatyeka for his help with the Xhosa, and I want to extend a special thank you to Loret Lundall. You have all been wonderful.

Thanks go also to Little, Brown and Company in New York for kindly allowing me the use of Nelson Mandela's beautiful quotes from *Long Walk to Freedom*.

And last, but certainly not least, thank you George, Smudge, Mommy, Boytjie, Shoggy, Fabian and Akeira, my ever-present cosy and loving companions. Your loyalty is much appreciated!

Fransje van Riel

The day begins …

'Two o'clock in the morning, when the women wake up, this we call *ukukhala kweenkuku zokuqala*, the first crowing of the roosters. Three o'clock in the morning, when the women gather firewood and water, this we call *ukukhala kweenkuku zesibini*, the second crowing of the roosters. Four o'clock in the morning, when everyone wakes up and has the coffee the women have made, this we call *ukukhala kweenkuku zesithathu*, the third crowing of the roosters …'

– Nomfusi Vinah Yekani

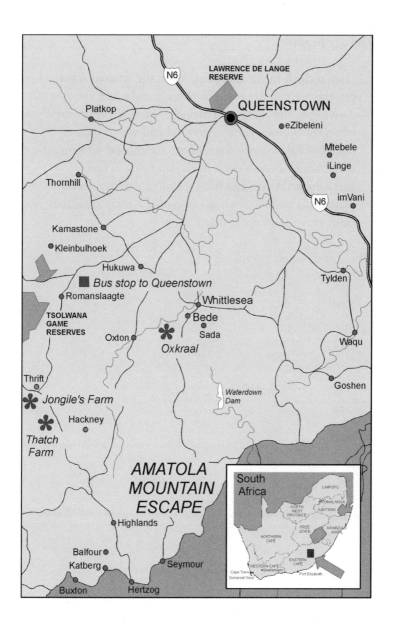

Election Day
27 April 1994

That day, I remember it so well. The people, the excitement, the singing. It made me feel strong emotions. Of relief. And of utmost joy.

Tata Madiba had been out of prison for four years, and now the day had finally come. We black people were going to vote. I was fifty-five years old when all this happened in 1994, a Xhosa woman in her middle years who had never been able to speak out for her country. We had for many years sung the songs and thought the thoughts, but never before had we had the power to steer our country in the direction of our choice. But this day, we were doing just that.

Not being able to vote was just one of the many ways we had suffered under apartheid, that hated policy of the white man. And black people were not the only ones that suffered. Our country was torn into many pieces – the white areas, the Coloured areas and those for the Indians. There were rules and laws for everything; signs dividing us everywhere. '*Net Blankes*, Whites Only.' We were told to carry around a Pass wherever we went and for whatever we wanted to do. We used to call these *dompasses*, because they were supposed to keep us dumb.

During the worst years, I could not go anywhere without permission stamped in this Pass. Without it, you did not even exist. You could just as well be dead.

Of course, in the rural areas during the earlier years it was not so bad. Our lives carried on much as they always had, fetching water from the river, collecting firewood and herding the cattle back from the fields to the kraal at the end of the day. But in the cities it was very, very bad. Many men had left their wives and children in the rural areas to look for work. The cities gave you little or no money, but plenty of despair and loneliness. And burning anger, hidden behind silent defeat.

So that beautiful morning of 27 April 1994 was very important. I was going to cast my vote, and it was going to count.

It was a very exciting moment, but also a little strange. As a sign of my respect for Tata Mandela, I put on my *umbhaco*, my traditional African dress and headgear. This dress was a very beautiful red, made from a thick material embroidered with all sorts of symbols. I only used to put it on for special occasions like weddings, births in our family or funerals. Or a day like today, my day to vote for Tata Madiba.

'Grace,' I said to my friend, 'we are voting for a good and brave man, a man who made a promise to our people that he will never break. So we must try and look our very best.'

Grace, like me, also worked as a domestic, for the family next door. We often got together for a cup of tea after we had finished work, and this morning she had come to my room so that we could walk to the polling station together. It was a cold morning. Really! It was very chilly, and still dark and misty. The Cape winter was on its way.

As I locked my room, I heard the little bird that had made its nest in the camellia bush that grew next to my door. It was a little Cape white-eye, a pretty little bird with a white ring around its eye. I saw it, flicking its small wings so excitedly, as if it knew why this day was so special. We started walking down the path and this little white-eye followed us a bit, singing a sweet song. I stopped and looked at it again and smiled. We, too, were going to spread our wings today.

Despite the early hour, there were a lot of people making their way towards the polling station. Grace and I looked at each other, our eyes shining and so happy. In the distance, we heard a group of women ululating and we joined in.

By the time we got there, there were people everywhere. It was like being in the middle of an ant colony. People were coming from all directions. A minibus taxi spilled a group of young men on the far side of the Somerset West town hall. An elderly white couple parked their car at the main entrance and walked slowly to the end of the queue. Others came on foot.

Dawn broke over the Hottentots Holland Mountains as we joined the long line of voters. As I stood there, the sun rising over their jagged peaks, I was reminded of the morning sun as it rolled over the mountains at my home near the Transkei border. And how, as a child, I would sit and watch the landscape catch fire. For just a moment, I was home again, and I heard the chorus of a song in the distance.

'*Afrika! Afrika! Afrika!*'

Too soon, my memories faded, and it was the Hottentots Holland Mountains in front of me again. Seeing all these people with their smiling faces on the morning of that voting day made me feel something that is very difficult to describe. I felt so peaceful and warm. I remember thinking, *This is how a newborn feels as it looks into its mother's eyes and opens its heart so wide that it reflects the smile it sees on her face.*

It was a good thing we had come so early, because soon there were hundreds of men and women in that line. I later found out that it was like that across the whole country. Pictures taken from the air on that day showed long queues snaking around buildings, roads and fields like giant songololos. Never before had I known a morning like this.

The noise and laughter reminded me of my home again. Of a time that was filled with happiness, when I was growing up with Mama. Without even thinking about it, I closed my eyes again.

I was home. Sitting on top of the mountain among the grass and the willow trees, with the valley down below me and the rocks at my feet, I could hear the birds singing and see the baboons as they sat on the cliffs. Their barks rang out across the hills as they sat drinking in the first rays of sunshine, as if to say, 'Welcome, sun. We were cold without you in the night.'

Mama and I were there together, out in the hills just before dawn, watching the light orange sun rise. It was that peaceful time of day when the sun peeped over the mountain into a new day. And as it did, the baboons, dark shapes upon the rocks, began moving towards their roosting tree.

I opened my eyes and sighed.

Those days were long gone, and my home was far from where I now stood with Grace, waiting to vote. By 1994, I had lived in Somerset West for nearly thirty years, longer even than what I lived at home. Many of those years I was not welcome as a Xhosa woman without a Pass book. I had to hide from the authorities. And I had to lie. Apartheid made me a liar. But after this day, I would not have to lie any longer.

I asked Grace to stand in front of me in the queue. It wasn't because I was scared. It was just that I could not believe that this was really happening. That we were really going to vote. As I took her place, I saw that a very nice-looking white lady was in the queue behind us. She kept looking at Grace and me as we chatted in a way that made me feel a little bit uncomfortable. Then she started talking to us in Xhosa.

'I understand your language, you know,' she said. Grace and I must have looked very surprised, because then the woman smiled. 'I am sorry if I startled you. Please, relax. Today is the day we fix all the things that have been wrong in this country for so long.'

I was so overwhelmed at what this white lady had said that I didn't know what to say. But Grace knew. 'Madam!' she said, '*usithetha kamnandi isiXhosa!* You speak very good Xhosa, Madam!'

As we stood in that queue, we spoke more to that lady and found out that she had grown up on a farm north of East London. That was where she learnt our language. It was strange to hear her speak like a Xhosa, but also very nice.

As we left the voting station, we were stopped by many people who were still waiting in the queue. They wanted to know what it had been like. They spoke quietly, asking for which party we had voted. But I did not want to tell them.

'That is my secret,' I said.

My madam at the time, Mrs Philips, was a very kind lady and had given me the whole day off. She told me that this was a very special day for South Africa, and that I must go and enjoy myself after making my cross. So Grace and I went to my cousin, who had a room in a hostel just outside Somerset West, to celebrate the day with him and some others. He had cooked a meal of pap and stew for us, and after lunch we sat outside, drinking wine and African beer and chatting about the elections.

We all knew that Tata Madiba was going to win. Everybody was laughing and talking about what was going to happen after he was president. One of my cousin's friends spoke very loudly and waved his hands about.

'I am going to own the home and shop of my *baas*,' he shouted.

'You will never get that house,' my cousin told him.

'Oh, yes I will,' he said. 'I will own that house. He will go and live overseas and then it will all be mine.'

We all laughed and told him he was dreaming. By the time we stopped laughing I saw that the woman sitting next to my cousin was crying softly. When we asked her what was wrong, she said she was crying because she was so happy.

'Now I know for sure that they will never bring back the Pass laws,' she said. 'I will never have to sleep in the bushes again.'

This made us laugh again and she also started laughing. I think she had a bit much to drink, but it didn't matter. Today was a good and happy day. We all deserved to indulge. The mist over our country had lifted and the sun had broken through to shine on us all. It was a day for Africans.

It was a day for Africa.

As I sat there, with all the people talking around me, I started to think about my life again. About my husband and my children. And my mother. Mama.

The memories came flooding back again. I saw the rolling hills of the eastern Cape Province in front of me and the peaks of the mountains pointing to the blue sky. I saw the bushes and the thorn trees whistling and waving in the wind. The crickets hummed along with the rush of the endless gurgling river.

I heard the mooing of the cattle and laughed at the chickens bickering over dried mealies. And there was my home! A round hut of mud and stones and cow dung, like one of many mushrooming in the field. Smoke came from the windows. I smelt *isidudu* and *imithwane*, mealie-meal pap and pumpkin-and-runner-bean stew that my mother used to make and that I used to love so much.

I saw her right there, too. In her long dress and her *doek* around her short black hair. She was smiling at me, like she used to do. Mama.

I was back there. Back home. And I was that happy child again.

Part 1

First crowing
1943 to 1959

'I was not born with a hunger to be free. I was born free – free in every way that I could know. Free to run into the fields near my mother's hut, free to swim in the clear stream that ran through my village, free to roast mealies under the stars and ride the broad backs of slow-moving bulls. As long as I obeyed my father and abided by the customs of my tribe, I was not troubled by the laws of man or God.'

Nelson Rolihlahla Mandela
Long Walk to Freedom, 1994

1

My blessed childhood

Dawn always comes early to my home in Oxkraal, breathing hazy light before the angry African sun sweeps over the hills. This special time of the morning, when it is no longer night but not yet quite day, does not last long at all. It is a whisper, a moment in time that I have always loved.

I was born in this beautiful area a long time ago, in 1943. As a young child, I used to wait outside Mama's rondavel, watching for those first golden rays to spill over the mountaintops. Then that big, red ball of fire would rise, spreading an orange glow over the valleys like an eagle stretching its massive wings. It lit the grasses and the trees, the early birds and all those things that were around me. Without the sun, the river did not sparkle and the birds did not sing quite so beautifully. Each new day was a time of promise, a new beginning.

During the rainy season, thick mist sometimes blocked the sun. But the beauty of the morning would still be there. A thin layer of dew would cover all those bushes and trees, like the veil of a young bride in church. I can still feel that cool, gentle dew on my fingertips.

We lived in a traditional round hut in the middle of a sloping field. Its thick walls were made from mud and well-crushed stones held together with cow dung, and these walls were capped by a roof of sun-streaked thatch.

The field we lived in was at the foot of two mountains. Two rivers ran on either side of it. The river that ran closest to the house was called the Umtha River. It came from the west and streamed to the east, in the direction of Whittlesea, and then headed south towards the ocean, keeping our world lush and green. The river attracted a lot of little insects, and these attracted the birds I loved so much.

When I was growing up, Whittlesea was a small village. Most of the people that lived there worked on the land, and most of the farms around it were owned by white people. The smallholding we lived on was far enough from Whittlesea for white people not to want to live there. It was on communal ground that was owned by one of the local chiefs. They had said that Mama could build her hut there after my father died, when she was looking for a place to stay.

We all knew that we were lucky to live in such a beautiful place, where the rivers brought us lots of fresh, clean water for the green vegetables that Mama grew. We also grew mealies on our sloping field. I used to love watching those mealies grow, waving to us from far away, showing off their juicy yellow corns.

These mealies gave us maize, which we used to make many different dishes. Mama often used to make *isidudu*, porridge, and *isonka samanzi*, steamed bread, which is very nice to eat. Or we would stamp the mealies and use them in a stew with beans and vegetables. We even made them into our special African beer, *umqombothi*, a drink much loved by everyone.

Many kinds of trees grew near the hut, hugging it with their branches as if it was a special place. There were mostly willow and thorn trees, but there were also other plants. Wild olive trees and aloes, and many different wild herbs. Mama used to make teas from these herbs, especially the aloes, nettle and African potato. Her teas were good medicine for colds, flus and even some infections. If she knew anyone who was sick she would go and visit them with tea to make them better, which is why everybody loved her so much. They called her *khuthala*, meaning a very diligent lady.

Mama raised us children to respect the old ways, telling us old African stories and teaching us Xhosa customs so that we would never forget where we came from. I was the last of many sisters and brothers, most of whom had, by the time I was old enough to know, moved away or died. In those days, a lot of babies and children died before they were old enough to have their own children. Even Mama lost four young ones, but that was a long time before I came to this world.

My oldest brothers and sisters were born many years before me and were already living with families of their own when Mama gave birth to me. When I was growing up, there were three of us still living with Mama: Ntsodo and Nomi, my sister and brother who were twins and about seven years older, and me. There was also Mziwakhe, Mama's first grandchild.

Back then, Whittlesea was a nice village, very clean with lots of trees and grass. Unfortunately, this has all changed. When I go home in December I see lots of rubbish on the streets. In the old days there was nothing like that. I feel a bit sad when I see that people have stopped caring.

The village was a little bit far from us, maybe four hours away on foot. There were about six shops, one police station, a magistrate's court, a garage, a bar and the post office. Only white people lived there; us black people were living further away in the rural areas or in the locations. The nearest locations were Shiloh and the Whittlesea location. A lot of people lived in the locations and worked in the village. And because there were only so many jobs in Whittlesea, a lot of young men went north to Queenstown to find work.

As a child, I was very happy that we didn't live in the location, because even though these places were nothing like those horrible, crowded squatter camps that I saw when I moved away to Cape Town years later, it was still a place where people lived very close to each other. No, no. Not for me. I loved the rural areas, where the wind brushed my short, curly black hair like a kind grandparent, and where the sun shone brightly on my face as I listened to the birds sing.

The best time for birdsong was in December, when many birds came from faraway places to my home in the far east of the Cape Province, right near the Transkei border. Our teachers told us that some of these birds had flown from Europe, where only white people lived. These birds were called swallows in English.

December was also the time of Christmas, which was my favourite time of the year. The weather was hot then, but it was also the rainy season, and we always felt fresh after a downpour cooled everything down. The rain cleaned all living things. The grass was greener afterwards, and the sky brighter. The thorn trees came out in bright yellow flowers, inviting insects and birds into their shoots.

During this time a special bird, which we called *phezu komkhono* because of the sound it made, used to visit our home. I don't know what the name of that bird is in English, but when we children heard it sing, we knew that Christmas was near. We would all laugh and shout, 'This bird says *Kresmesibhox, phezu komkhono*, which means "Our Christmas presents are near".'

It was a good time. Family members visited, and there was much singing and dancing. Sometimes our teachers arranged parties at our school, which was also the church. Everyone loved these parties.

Of course, Christmas was the time for presents. One December, Mama made a doll for me from material cut from an old apron and a blouse. I called it Nopopi and I would play with it for hours, which was probably a good thing as it kept me out of trouble.

Not that I was a naughty child. Mama often told us stories about children who didn't listen to their parents and ended up in jail. Sometimes they even died. One story I remember was about a young girl who died suddenly after saying she had a headache. When the elders gathered for her funeral, they were surprised to hear faint noises coming from the body and to see the blanket in which she was wrapped begin to move.

Shocked, some people ran away, probably thinking there was a ghost in the blanket. But when a few brave men looked a little closer they saw that the dead girl was not dead at all, but very much alive. Her father, who Mama said was a very nice old man, leaned over his daughter and listened carefully as she tried to speak. 'An angel told me to come back and ask for a *klap*,' this girl whispered, 'because you never gave me one when I did anything wrong. This angel did not like me because I was very naughty and I always made my parents' hearts sore. So please, Tata, give me a smack!'

So the father gave her a small smack with a thin stick that we call *uswazi*, after which she died, leaving her parents very unhappy because they felt that it had all been their fault.

That story really scared me! I told myself that I would never disobey Mama ever again.

Mama told us stories like this every night. They were meant to teach us wrong from right, but I knew that sometimes Mama would make them up if we children asked her about something she didn't want to answer. Like the time when my older sister gave birth, and we small children wanted to know where new babies came from. When we asked Mama, she told us that our sister had gone to the mountain in the night and there had been given a baby girl by a baboon. This was funny, especially since Mama was an excellent midwife. She delivered many babies for other people, and also for her own children. It was she who helped me deliver my first son, Wandile.

Mama was born in 1896 in Mkapusi, a small community close to Lady Frere in the Transkei, where many years later she met and married my father. After they were married, he and Mama moved to where his brother was staying in Hukuwa, a rural area slightly north and to the west of Whittlesea. They built a hut there, and farmed and had children, but then a terrible disease killed all the crops for two years in a row. After that, Mama and my father took my older brothers and sisters and left their home to look for work on white farms as far away as Graaff-Reinet in the Karoo.

Mama used to tell us smaller children how the family would spend weeks travelling with the few cows and sheep they had left, spending nights close to the road. Early in the mornings, my father would leave them there and walk to the closest farm to ask for work. If he got the job, he and his new employer would come back in a truck to fetch Mama, the children and the animals.

Only after my father died did Mama stop going from farm to farm and move to Oxkraal. By that time she was pregnant with me, and tired of moving from place to place.

'Nomfusi,' Mama always told me as I was growing up, 'we are very lucky to be living in this beautiful place where we can see the mountains and hear the birds in the trees. We have everything we need here, water from the river, firewood for cooking and healthy mealies for our samp.'

Nomfusi is my Xhosa name, meaning 'she who comes after twins', because I was born after my twin brother and sister, Ntsodo and Nomi. I have had many names in my lifetime. Nomfusi, Ntondo, Nowam, Vinah. Even Mary. Mama called me Nomfusi or Ntondo, which means 'the last one', because I was lastborn. My husband and in-laws called me Nowam. The teacher in school gave me my English name, Vinah. And the name Mary was given to me by Mr and Mrs Geldenhuys, the Afrikaans couple who were so good to me when I first came to Somerset West. They thought it would be safer for me to be called by a Coloured name than a Xhosa one because I didn't have a permit to work in the Cape and it would be better if the Pass inspectors thought I was Coloured.

But all of that happened many years later.

I loved Mama more than any other person in the world. She was a very attractive lady, and had a body that was not too fat or too skinny. Her complexion was light and she looked lovely in her traditional dress and headgear, going around barefoot.

She was also a strong woman. Looking back, I realise the reason we younger children never missed having a father was because we were never short of anything.

I remember Mama's voice, soft like a melody. I can almost hear her telling us stories as I got under the blankets with her at night. I slept with Mama until the day my husband came to take me away. Our bed was a mattress of empty mealie-meal bags filled with long grass cut from the river and dried in the sunshine.

I learnt everything I needed from Mama, even when she was already very old. She lived until she was almost one hundred years, passing away on 10 August 1989. It was very sad to see her strength grow weak and die, but at least she didn't suffer. She died peacefully in her sleep, on a Saturday night. I will never forget it.

Even today I miss her.

Mama had never seen much of the world, or even her own country. She had never gone further north than her home near Lady Frere, and she never travelled to the place I ran away to in 1966, to Somerset West. But that didn't mean that she didn't know the ways of the world. She was a very wise woman. And she never stopped loving me, not even when I ran away from my husband. I hated leaving her so far behind, but she knew why I had to leave. She never judged me.

There were many years between my oldest brother, Mabongo, and me. He was twenty-nine years old when I was just an *usana*, a small baby. He had left to look for work in Port Elizabeth, leaving his wife and small son with Mama, but he never came back. We never found out what happened to him. In time, his wife remarried. Her small son stayed with Mama. That was Mziwakhe.

My oldest sisters, Thwenya and Ntemntem, were born in 1916 and 1919. They both got married in traditional style when I was about one year old, and went on to live with their husbands and children in a small village on the other side of Queenstown. I don't remember their weddings; Mama told me about them only later. I don't really remember them living with us either, only that they used to sing lullabies for me when Mama was not home. '*Thula sana, thula mntwana,*' they sang. 'Hush baby, hush child! Mama is coming. She has gone to look for wood to cook for baby.'

Sometimes these lullabies were not so gentle. Sometimes they were threatening, like when my sisters sang, '*Thula sana, thula mntwana!* Hush baby, hush child! Here comes a baboon and it is going to eat you!'

Thwenya, my oldest sister, got married to a man who already had a wife, so she was regarded as *indlu yasekunene*, which means the right-hand house, or right-hand wife. Before they were married, her husband had given Mama six head of cattle for her. In our Xhosa tradition, a new husband must give his parents-in-law cattle as a symbol of his commitment to look after their daughter. That is lobola. Sometimes, lobola can also be a horse.

For a young man it can be quite difficult to pay this lobola and often his parents will help. It was the same in our family. Mama helped my brother Mabongo when he got married with his lobola – she gave three of Thwenya's cattle to the parents of my brother's bride. Ntemntem's four cattle were used as lobola for my brother, Solomon. Much later, all five of Nomi's went to pay for Mtshini because he made his girlfriend pregnant. Her name was Velisiwe. But he did not marry this girl. He married Nopinki and paid for her with the lobola given to Mama for me by my husband, Jongile.

After my sister Ntemntem came my brothers, Solomon and Mtshini, and then of course there were the twins, Nomi and Ntsodo. Solomon and Mtshini were eighteen and eleven years older than me, but, unlike Mabongo, they visited us quite often and this made us all very happy. We would all sit together and drink *amasi*, sour milk that is left to thicken until it is like yoghurt. We all liked this drink very much and we would take it together with the *mphokoqo*, cooked mealie meal.

I was very close to my brother Mtshini. He was a kind man, and a good older brother to me. He worked in Swellendam for a while and bought me my school uniform and shoes there, which he sent home in a parcel. They were the best shoes he could find. Polished and beautiful.

Mtshini was also very fond of Mama. Every time he came home for a holiday he would help her with the crops. If Mtshini visited us when the mealies were full and ripe in the fields, swaying under their heavy load, I would wake up in the mornings to the sound of thumping hoes as Mama and Mtshini were hard at work already, picking the mealies.

Mtshini died on 12 August 2002. He had been having problems with his heart for a short time, and this is what caused his death. We were all very sad to hear of his passing. At seventy-four years of age, he left behind a much-loved wife and eight children, six girls and two boys. And, of course, his brother and sisters.

But I jump ahead. There is still more to tell about my birthplace and all that happened there before I ran away to Somerset West.

When I was growing up, I was also very close to my brother Ntsodo and his twin sister, Nomi. They, in turn, were very fond of each other, even though they would sometimes fight terribly. Like the time when Ntsodo made coffee for Mama and me in the morning but not for his twin sister because, he said, she was lazy. When Nomi and Ntsodo fought, Mama would sometimes give them both a smack with a stick from the apple tree. After this hiding, Nomi would run away to Ntemntem, who was living on a white farm where her husband worked as a labourer. It was a full day's walk to that farm.

If Nomi hadn't come back after two days, Ntsodo would say, 'Mama, I want to go and fetch Nomi.' And he would walk to that farm and bring her back. By that time, everything would be forgotten – the fighting, the angry words that were said and the smack that Mama had given them with the stick from the apple tree. There would be laughing and hugging, and Mama would roll her eyes and say, 'Hmm, hmm. Now look at them! You would never guess that they were fighting before.'

And then there was me. Ntondo, the last one.

Across the river from our thatch-capped hut stood the mission school where I first went to school in the early 1950s. That was only a few years after Prime Minister D F Malan began apartheid. But we on the edge of the rural Transkei didn't notice all that much about those new laws and rules. It was much worse in the big towns and cities.

As a child, I liked school very much. It was my dream to become a teacher. The other job I wanted was to be a social worker. I would have liked something like that, a job where I could help other people.

As I said before, my school was also the old church, which stood to the north of my home across the Umtha River. Sometimes, in summer, there'd be so much rain drumming down from the skies that some of the school children couldn't cross the flooded river to get back home. This river filled up very quickly. I was always afraid of these heavy downpours because I wanted to go home after school to tell Mama what we had been learning that day. I hated being anywhere other than home.

I remember one such time. It had been a very hot day. All of us children were in the classroom, where the teacher was teaching us sums, when suddenly these big, black clouds started to grow outside. In minutes, the day had changed. We could no longer see the sun and it was very dark outside.

The teacher stopped writing on the blackboard and walked to the window, looking up at the sky. He could see that it was going to rain heavily very soon, so he clapped his hands to get our attention and said that all the children who had to cross the river to come to school were to run home as fast as possible.

There were about ten of us children who lived across the river, so we got up, said goodbye to the teacher and headed for the door. Just as I was leaving, the teacher stopped me and my friend, Nomakula, and said, 'Children, please. If you see the water moving down the river very fast, don't cross but come back to school and stay at one of the houses close by for the night. I don't want you to be swept away by the water and drowned.'

I looked at my friend before answering my teacher because the last thing I wanted was to spend the night at someone else's house. I just wanted to go home. But, seeing that my teacher was serious, I said, 'Yes, teacher.'

'Good. Now *run*.'

The river was about fifteen minutes' walk from the school. By the time Nomakula and I reached the windmill near the water's edge, it had begun to thunder. In the distance I saw a bolt of lightning hit the silent earth as if it had done something terribly wrong.

The teacher had been right to send us home. The river was filling up very quickly. As we stood there, not knowing what to do, I saw Mama and Ntsodo as small dots on the horizon, running towards us. They reached the other side of the river a few minutes later. By that time, the water was wild and strong. Mama started waving her arms over head, shouting at me.

'Nomfusi! Don't cross! You must not cross! The river is already flooded, and the water is going very fast. *Go back*!'

Mama knew me so well! She knew that I would have tried to get across that angry river if she had not come to warn me. To tell me not to be foolish.

Then Ntsodo also called out. 'I can swim across and fetch you, Nomfusi.'

But this made Mama very angry. '*No!* No, my children!' she shouted. 'That is too dangerous. The river will kill you both. Nomfusi, turn back! Go to the house of the headman and ask him and his wife if you can stay the night with them! You too,

Nomakula! I will tell your mother that you will not be coming home tonight!'

The other children whose homes were on the other side had already gone back to the school, but I just stood there because I did not want to stay at the headman's house. Mama was waving her arms impatiently now.

'Now, Nomfusi! Run! *Balekani imvula enkulu sele ifikile!* The rain is getting nearer!'

Nomakula and I had no choice but to turn back and run as fast as we could. I was very upset, crying even. The lightning was very scary and we were both getting very wet from the rain. By the time we reached the headman's home, we were soaked.

'*Yo, nimanzi!*' the headman said when he opened the door. He was one of the few people I knew who was wealthy enough to live in a house with different rooms, and not a traditional hut. 'You are both very wet! Is the river already full, my children?'

We were welcomed. The headman's son, a boy of about sixteen, made a warm fire in one of the rooms and left us alone so that we could take off our clothes to dry. We covered ourselves with the warm, thick blankets that had been left for us and sat down in front of the roaring logs. Nomakula and I looked at each other and smiled. We were thankful that the headman had taken us into his home and had been so kind to us. Already we were feeling a lot happier.

After a supper of mashed potatoes, pumpkin and mealie meal, we talked about how lucky we were to have been taken in from the rain. It was also good that we were together. Nomakula was my best friend and also a relative. Her mother was the daughter of my mother's brother.

When we woke the next morning, the new day was very different to the one before. The rain had stopped and the sky was a happy blue, with only a few white clouds that looked like sheep. We thanked the headman and his wife and son for looking after us so well and went straight to school.

I was so happy that the sun was out again! By the time we finished school that day, the river had gone down a lot and Nomakula and I knew it was going to be easy to cross without any problems. Mama was also happy to have me home again. She hugged and kissed me and told me that I had been a good girl for going to the headman's house. She then made a fire, letting the flames die down so that she could roast some nice juicy mealies over the heat. It was a special supper to celebrate that I was home again. We used to call those mealies *umbhona owojiweyo*. Roast mealie cob. I can still smell those yellow mealies as we turned them until they were blistered and brown all around.

I had been away only one short day, but already I had missed these trees and the fields and the crops and the birds. This was my home. This was where I belonged.

And I didn't want to be anywhere else in the world.

2

Me singing the Malan song in school

One Friday in October, when I was about eleven years old, our school principal said that there was going to be a concert at the school, and that pupils from other schools in the area had been invited to join in.

'Six other schools will attend the concert,' beamed our principal, Mr Thekanti. We were all very excited to hear the news and clapped our hands together.

On the day of the concert, we went home after school to change into the uniforms we wore only on special occasions. This uniform was made up of a white shirt, black dress, black belt and shoes. The boys wore a white shirt and black shorts. I remember feeling excited about singing in the senior choir, knowing that I would be standing in the front row where everybody would see me.

Back at school, everyone was chatting, laughing, looking at the children from the other schools and waiting for the concert to start. Our school was the first to sing, straight after the prayers, and we sang a beautiful, clear song. After us came a school from Queenstown, and their teacher told everybody to join his choir in singing the next song:

'Iyakunyathel' iAfrika
Malan lumka wanyathelwa
Iyakunyathel' iAfrika
Malan lumka wanyathelwa
Malan lumka wanyathelwa!'

And the chorus would follow:

'Afrika! Afrika! Afrika!'

It was about the prime minister, D F Malan, and the meaning of the song was:

'Africa will thump you
Malan beware
Africa will stamp on you
Malan beware
Malan beware!
This is our *Afrika! Afrika! Afrika!*'

Everybody sang along. The teachers and the parents and soon us children joined in, too, repeating the words over and over again. As we were singing this song, the parents and teachers raised their right fists up in the air. And each time we sang it, our voices grew louder and our fists grew harder until the whole school hall was shaking with the sound. It was all very exciting.

I remember not really understanding the meaning of the song or why we sang it with our fists held high. My friend Nomakula and I asked the other school children what the words meant. They explained that the song was about Bantu education. They told us that we black children were only receiving a little bit of schooling, not nearly as much as white children, and that Prime Minister Malan wanted to keep it that way. He wanted black people to be uneducated so that they would not question the white man.

So that was what Bantu education meant! I did not know that. And neither did Nomakula. We looked at each other and began to giggle, and then we joined the chorus again when it started singing. '*Afrika! Afrika! Afrika!*'

The teachers did not like this Bantu education at all. The teachers didn't like apartheid. And they didn't like Malan.

Dr D F Malan had won the election in 1948, when I was just five years old. Once he became prime minister, this white man began enforcing all these new rules on black people, telling us where we could live, who we could marry, and what kind of jobs we could have. He didn't like black people to live with the white people. But I only learnt about that later.

We did not have this kind of trouble in Oxkraal in 1954, but many people in other parts of the country were having a terrible time. And it kept getting worse as the years went by. In the late 1950s, thousands of people were forced to leave the places that had been their homes their whole lives. I had never before heard about this District Six, but by the end of the decade everybody was talking about it. We also started hearing other unfamiliar names, of places and people. Sharpeville, Alexandria. Verwoerd, Strijdom, and, increasingly, a man named Mr Mandela.

But that day, at school, none of us children knew of these things. Still, we liked to sing the song anyway.

The concert went on until early the next morning. By this time we were all very tired. The children from the Queenstown school still had to go home by bus, a drive that would take about another hour. I felt for them. They would be so tired by the time they got home. Luckily for me, it took only twenty minutes to walk home.

When I got home, Mama was waiting for me outside. When she saw me coming down the road with four of my friends, she waved to us.

'Nomakula, Nomsa, Ncediswa, Nomvula!' she called. 'All of you girls must come along with me to Nomsa's house. You too, Nomfusi!'

We were not surprised at Mama's request and giggled because we knew what was going to happen. It took us about another fifteen minutes of walking before we reached Nomsa's rondavel. We were whispering all the way.

When we arrived, Nomsa's mother came out to greet us. She took us to a different rondavel, where we were told to wait. Inside this hut we saw several elderly African women sitting on the floor. They showed us to sit down, and began to ask us questions.

'Girls,' one of the women began, 'have you been with any boyfriends at the concert? Tell the truth now!'

'No, Mama Nzolo,' we said together.

'One of your school friends is going to have a baby,' Mama Nzolo told us, frowning deeply. 'So now we are going to talk about the old ways to prevent you girls from getting pregnant without being married.'

We looked at each other.

'Those of you who have a boyfriend must listen very carefully,' said Mama Nzolo. 'If that boy says he wants to touch your private parts, you must not agree. You must end that relationship right away.'

We nodded respectfully. 'Yes, Mama.'

Having said her piece, Mama Nzolo nodded that she was ready to find out if we were still pure. In those days, this was tradition. We were told to take off our uniforms. One by one, Mama Nzolo looked inside us to see if we had been with a boy.

If she found a girl who was no longer pure, she would tell the mother of the girl, who would then tell that girl's father. Then both parents would go to the father and mother of the boy. If he confessed to sleeping with the girl, his parents would have to pay one goat to that girl's family as punishment. If the girl became pregnant, the parents of the boy would also be told, and they would have to pay five head of cattle for that girl's virginity.

We thought nothing of it, of taking off our clothes and having Mama Nzolo look inside us. We knew this was a custom, a tradition of our people. I think that we even felt a little proud. We were young women, after all.

Today, of course, this sort of thing does not happen so much anymore. Young women nowadays lead such different lives to us. Back then, this test was all part of growing up. And, of course, my friends and I had nothing to be scared of, for the last thing on our minds in those years was to be with a man. We had a whole lifetime ahead for that.

Or so we thought.

One day, not long after we sang the Malan song, another concert was held at our school. This time it was put together by the church to raise money. I will never forget that concert because something happened that day that gave me and my friends a very big shock.

It was a Monday evening, and when we arrived at the church it was already full of people. The celebrations were going well. Several sheep had been killed and the church ladies prepared the meat for us all. At about nine o'clock everybody was given food. The meat was served with rice, samp, mealies, potatoes, green vegetables, everything. After supper, it was time for the children from the different schools to sing, and after that the party carried on all the way through the night.

Just before sunrise, the school principal asked some of the children to fetch fresh water from the windmill at the river for the ladies who were cooking breakfast at the mission. He told five of us to go. I was one of them, and so was Nomakula.

It was already a very beautiful morning. The sky was clear and the last of the bright stars were out. Looking at those stars against the sky as black as ink made Nomakula and me think about faraway places, places even further than those shining stars. We skipped along, singing a beautiful song about the morning star. It was the same song that we had sung at the concert, to which everybody had clapped their hands. It went like this:

'*Laphuma ikhwezi*
Laphum' ikhwezi lokusa
Ikhwezi

Ntombi yezulu khanyisa
Khanyisa ntombi yezulu.'

This means:

> 'There appears the morning star
> There appears the morning star
> The star, the star, daughter of the sky!
> Light, light, daughter of the sky!
> There comes the crack of dawn,
> Beautiful morning star.'

It felt so good to sing this song at the birth of a new day.

After we had fetched the water from the river and given it to the women cooking at the mission, which was basically a house with four rooms, we were met by the reverend who told us to wait for him in the hall while he went into his office. The reverend was a Xhosa man, short and old, who was married to a very nice lady. At the time, she was working as a nurse in different hospitals in the Cape Province. She only now and then came home to visit her husband.

As we stood there waiting, the reverend appeared again. '*Molweni, mantombi.* Hello, girls,' he said. 'Now you must come inside my office, one by one, so that I can thank you properly for your kindness!'

Nomakula was the first to go inside. The reverend closed the door behind her. 'Come, Nomakula,' we heard his deep voice say inside the room. 'I will give you some sweets for bringing the water to the ladies.'

But we did not hear Nomakula reply. Everything was quiet. One of the other girls (she was quite a naughty one) peeped through the keyhole to see what was happening inside.

'What is it?' we asked her, but before she said anything, she let out a very big gasp. Then she started to giggle softly. 'What is going on in there?' we asked again. All of us girls were now beginning to feel very curious.

'Shhh!' she hissed, turning to us.

Then the door opened and Nomakula came out of the room, giggling. She walked straight past us, tucking a few sweets in the pocket of her special uniform.

The reverend's deep voice boomed across the mission hall. 'Next!'

I was the last to go inside that room. I remember shaking as I went in and saw the reverend's smile as he closed the door behind me. I did not like the way his eyes were looking at me, not at all.

'Come closer, Nomfusi!'

As I shuffled forwards, this man took a big handful of toffees from a trunk and held them out to me. When I was close enough, he pulled me towards him. I said nothing. 'There, there, Nomfusi,' he said as he stuffed those colourfully wrapped sweets in the pocket of my short dress. 'That is to thank you for bringing the water.'

Then, with his other hand, the reverend went under my dress, pushing his shaking thick fingers all the way up until they were right between my legs. Pulling me close to his heavy body, he started kissing me. The next moment his mouth was inside mine, cold and wet. It didn't last long, but it was enough for me to want to run away from that man as fast as I could.

I didn't know what to do! What was going on? All I knew was that I wanted to get out of this room and get far away from this horrible man with his horrible hands.

As we left the mission, the reverend waved us goodbye. 'Thank you, girls,' he said loudly. 'Thank you for the water.'

We were all in such a state of shock that we didn't know what to say to each other. 'How can the reverend kiss us like that?' one of the girls eventually asked. 'With his big hand touching us?'

But no one had the answer.

That was the first time I was kissed like that. I did not like it, not at all, and I felt quite sick. When we got to the windmill,

I knelt down to wash my face, rinsing my mouth over and over again. I was in tears.

We didn't talk much for the rest of the way home, not even to say goodbye. We had never thought, not for a second, that the reverend would do this sort of thing. After all, he was a holy man, old and respected.

I couldn't tell anyone about it, not even Mama. I was too shy and afraid that I had done something wrong. And I couldn't stand to look at the sweets he had given me. I hated them. Even to this day I can hear the sound of those wrappers in my pocket. In the end, I just threw them away in the bushes.

The following day in school, the other girls also said that they did not tell their families. We were all too scared to talk about it. But we knew that what the reverend had done was wrong.

Not long after that, something changed in my body one morning at school. Mama never told me about these things, but my friends and I had heard some of the older girls in school talking about the time when a girl first starts to bleed.

'Please, sir,' I said. 'May I go outside?'

My teacher said yes, asking me if anything was wrong. I think he saw that I was not my usual self, but I wasn't going to tell *him* what I thought was happening! So I told him that I was alright.

'Welekazi,' I said to the girl sitting next to me in class, '*Nceda, ndikhaphe siye phandle.* Please come with me outside.'

We walked out of the classroom and found a spot behind the bushes where no one could see us. This was the same place where we went to have a wee. There, I saw that I was right.

I had become a woman.

'What are you going to do, Nomfusi?' Welekazi asked softly.

'I am going home.'

She walked back to the classroom with me. I told my teacher that my stomach was now sore. He told me I could go home, and I packed my books and left.

When I got home, Mama was inside the hut weaving a mat. She looked very surprised to see me home so early.

'*Yintoni mntwana wam? Sesiphumile isikolo?*' she asked. 'What is it, my child? Is the school out already? I did not look at the sun. What time is it?'

When I showed her what had happened, Mama took some pieces of flannel material and quickly sewed them together. 'Don't cry, my child,' she said when she saw the tears coming. 'You are a woman now. Every woman comes to this time.'

She then gave me the wad of material and told me how to use it. She explained that, from this time on, I could not drink *amasi* or eat eggs or chicken on the seven days of my womanhood. Mama also told me that I was to wash at the river, but, after this time, I could eat eggs and chicken and drink *amasi* again, and also wash inside the hut. This was the custom.

Early one Saturday a month later, a young sheep was slaughtered to let the ancestors know that I had become a woman. At the celebration, Ntsodo also plucked a few hairs from the tail of the cow of the home.

The cow of the home is very important in our culture. It is never sold or killed for meat, as it belongs to the ancestors. It is so important that a herd boy may not even throw stones at it to stop it going into the crop fields. This cow is called *inkomo yobulunga,* and it is loved by all the family.

The cow of the home also helps in family matters. If a daughter gets married and doesn't fall pregnant by her husband, a hair will be pulled from the tail of that cow and put around her neck as a charm. She will then get pregnant.

On the Saturday when we celebrated me becoming a woman, Mama took the hairs that Ntsodo had plucked from the cow and rolled them on her leg before weaving them into a necklace. I was told to wear this necklace until it broke and to eat the meat from the young sheep that had been slaughtered. That was tradition.

I had entered a new phase in life. That of a young woman.

3

Mama's deep dark cloud of sorrow

One morning, when I was about fifteen years old, I came home from school and found Mama sitting in the shade of the huge thorn tree close to our home. It was a hot and sticky January day, and the walk from school had made me feel tired.

'*Molo, Mama!*' I always loved the time after school, when Mama and I would sit together in the shade of the tree, talking about all the things I had been taught that day.

Mama had never been to school, but she needed no teaching to be a very clever person. Creative, too. Even though she didn't have a sewing machine, she made dresses for me and Nomi, all by hand. She even made clothes for other people. Her dresses were very beautiful, covered with all sorts of colourful beads. She also wove baskets for collecting sweet mealies.

Once, Mama even made a whole scarecrow! It was a time when the crops were ripe enough to give us wheat, but the birds kept flying in to eat the seeds. Ntsodo asked Mama to make a scarecrow to keep the birds away.

Mama made this scarecrow from an old pair of Ntsodo's trousers. When it was ready, she took an old hat and put that on top, and then dressed it in a jacket. Together, Mama and Ntsodo carried it into the field.

Chuku, our dog, had never seen a scarecrow in his life and didn't know what to make of it. He didn't know whether to be scared of it and run away, or to attack it. So he just started jumping around it, barking all the time. He then charged straight at it, tearing at its clothes and almost shredded the scarecrow to pieces! It was very funny, and it made me laugh so much that it hurt my stomach.

Mama did not think it was funny, not at all.

'Nomfusi! Stop laughing! If you laugh again I am going to take your nice dresses and make another scarecrow out of *them*!'

I stopped immediately. 'Yes, Mama.'

She called Chuku to her, and he came immediately, looking very proud of himself.

Chuku was a very nice dog. A male, brownish in colour and with a curved tail that pointed back to his head. I don't think he was any one breed. He stayed with us for many years and we were all very fond of him. When he died of snakebite, we all cried for him.

When Chuku saw a cobra, he would bark and bark and bark, and when that cobra reared up high, he would attack like lightning, catching the snake by the neck and shaking it hard before throwing it far away. If that did not kill the snake, he would do this again and again until it did. We used to run away if we saw Chuku with a snake, because we were scared that when he tossed the snake away it would land on us.

Chuku used to be a very good snake-killer. Yes, he was very clever with them, but not the day he died. That day, the snake won and we lost our very dear friend.

We also had a cat, Nori, who I loved very much. She was very pretty and she had a lovely character. Her fur was golden and, like Chuku, she used to catch snakes in front of the house. Nori always slept with me and Mama, on top of our blankets inside the house.

Sometimes, when something happened to make me feel unhappy, I would walk to the river and sit on a big rock to be by myself. Sometimes I'd cry, and every time this happened I would feel Nori rub her soft, lean body against my leg. Chuku would do the same. Those two were great friends. After they said hello to me they would play together, and just watching them was enough for me to stop feeling sad. I'd forget my troubles and laugh and clap my hands at their games.

But I must go back to that afternoon when I came out of school to find Mama so unhappy. This day, there was no happy talking about what I had done in school while we watched the chickens scratching in the yard. This day was different.

'What is wrong, Mama?' I cried as I sat down next to her under that thorn tree.

But she just shook her head. 'No, don't worry Nomfusi. I am fine. I was just lost in thought.'

I could see that this was not true, so I asked again. But she would not say anything. 'Go inside, Nomfusi. Get yourself something to eat. There is some steamed bread inside the black pot.'

Normally I would be hungry after I got home from school, but now, seeing Mama like that, I was not hungry at all. Something was wrong and she was not telling me what it was. I wondered if it was something I had done. I looked at her again but couldn't tell. She looked away from me and stared down at the sewing on her lap. She was trying to hold back her tears.

Now I was also beginning to feel tearful. Seeing this, Mama said, 'Don't worry, my daughter. I will tell you. Just give me a moment.'

So I went to help Mziwakhe, Mama's first grandson and my nephew, herd our few cattle and sheep into the kraal where they stayed during the night. By this time, Ntsodo was working in Queenstown and Nomi was married to a man who worked on a dairy farm, so when I made supper after helping Mziwakhe I needed to make only enough for the three of us. That evening, we ate thick mealiepap with green vegetables on top.

In all this time, Mama still had not said anything at all, and we ate the meal in silence. Only after Mziwakhe and I had cleaned the dishes and come back inside the house again did Mama speak.

'Listen, children,' she said. 'I am old now. And I am feeling a deep, dark cloud of sorrow inside of me, such as I have never felt before in my life.'

Mziwakhe and I held our breaths. I had never heard Mama speak like that before. Mziwakhe and I knew something very big was going to come. Poor Mama. She was trying so hard not to cry, and to be strong for us.

'Bring me some water, Nomfusi,' she whispered.

I was now sobbing quietly because I feared the worst of things to come. But I did as she asked and fetched some water. After she had taken a few sips, she said, 'The headman sent a committee member this morning to bring bad news to all the people in this area.' She paused a moment, before looking me straight in the eye.

'All the people on this side of the river must move across and build new houses for themselves.' As she was speaking, a tear escaped from her eye and rolled slowly down her right cheek. 'I must leave my beautiful smallholding. *We* must leave our beautiful smallholding. Our home.'

'But why, Mama, why?' I was now crying uncontrollably. The news was even worse than I could have imagined.

'Please, don't let them take it, Mama!' said Mziwakhe. He had always called his grandmother Mama. 'It is yours! No one can take your home away from you!'

'No, my children,' Mama said, her voice growing stronger now the bad news was out. 'The headman who owns the land has said we must move. We are no longer allowed to live here. We have been given a year to get everything together and to make our move.' She wiped away another tear, straightened her back and tried to smile. 'I am sure everything is going to be all right,' she said. 'Things change. That is the way life is. And we must change with it.'

We weren't so sure. Our home was everything to us. The

idea of leaving it, and its birds and trees and valleys, was too much to bear.

But we had no say in the matter. Even though we would be allowed to keep some cattle there, we were not allowed to live there anymore.

A week passed, and then another and another. Life sort of went back to normal, making us forget about having to leave. But then, about ten months later, Mr Thekanti, my school principal, arrived at our house on horseback. It was a beautiful November day, warm and lovely as early summer mornings used to be at my home.

I was inside the kraal, milking the cows and listening to the lovely song of birds, when I heard the sound of galloping hooves from the crop field in front of our home. Mziwakhe was herding the sheep to the fields, and I noticed that Chuku, our dog, was lying at the gate of the kraal, watching me.

Nori was nowhere to be seen. Maybe she was hunting, or frightened by the sounds of the horse. But not Chuku! When that dog heard the galloping he jumped up and ran towards the horse, barking the whole time. Mziwakhe tried to call Chuku back, and as he did I got up to see who was coming.

My hand shot before my mouth. *Hayi! Nkosi yam nguti-tshala omkhulu!* Oh, no! It's my school principal! What was he doing here?

I knew that this teacher would not like to have a dog barking at him like that. Chuku would be in big trouble! Not wanting to get in trouble myself, I decided to stay put with the cows and wait to hear what happened.

After a little while, I took another look and saw that Mama had come outside to shoo Chuku away. The principal got off the horse, took out his pipe and lit it without looking at Mama. Just then, Chuku let out one last loud bark, giving the principal such a fright that his pipe dropped from his mouth and fell on the ground next to the horse's legs.

I giggled.

Mama knew I was watching and decided to ignore both me and the lost pipe. She greeted my principal.

'*Molo*. Are you coming in, teacher?'

Ignoring her invitation, the principal said, 'Nose, I have arrived here as a committee member to tell you that the time has come for you to move to the other side of the river. By January you must be gone.'

That was all that my principal said. He didn't come inside and drink *amasi* with Mama first or even console her after telling her the news, even though he knew how much she loved her smallholding. Instead, he got back on his horse, touched the tip of his hat and rode off, looking back over his shoulder at Chuku as the dog ran after the horse for a bit.

Mama sat down, her face a funny grey colour. She was close to tears.

'Oh, Mama,' I said. 'Don't cry! It's going to be all right.' I repeated this over and over, trying to comfort her, but I don't think I did a very good job.

'Oh, no, my child,' she wailed. 'Not this time! It is not going to be all right! We have to leave our beautiful small-holding! I never thought I would have to move again. Not after all those times I moved with your father from farm to farm, working so hard for a living. I am old now. I don't want to move again.' I didn't know what to say. She continued. 'Ever since January, when I heard the bad news, I hoped it would all be forgotten. But now the moment has come.'

I just stood there. I had never seen Mama so unhappy. Mziwakhe also looked very sad and I could see that he was keeping unusually quiet.

We were given two months to move, and those two months went by quickly. I never knew that time could go that fast. We sent letters to my older brothers and sisters, telling them what was happening. Ntsodo took leave from his job in Queenstown and came home to help us with the move. His usually friendly face looked hard and tired when he arrived.

'When I left to look for work, I thought I would always be able to come back to this home again,' he told me on his first night home. 'It looks like I was wrong.'

We had to go. We left our much loved home very early on a Friday morning just as it was getting light. The green grass and bushes were covered in a fine, cool dew. The birds were already singing. All these wonderful things that used to make me so happy. But not this morning.

We had packed all our belongings, plus the chickens, Chuku and Nori, on the ox wagon, where I too sat. Holding a stick, Mama helped Mziwakhe and Ntsodo round up the cattle, sheep and goats. I remember having a strong feeling of fear. I was leaving the only home I had ever known. Could I ever be happy again?

But there was nothing to be done about it. It was time to go. Mama climbed up on the ox wagon next to me and, at her command, the animals pulled the wagon forward. With a lurch, it was taking us away from the place we loved so much. We were all weeping.

Ntsodo walked next to the cattle as they pulled the wagon, occasionally cracking his whip on the ground to spur them on. He loved these animals, calling them by their names. I don't remember all their names, but I do remember that there was one very big black bull. His name was Nomyayi, which means 'black crow'. Then there was Donker, a dark brown bull, and Wit Voet, an impressive dark animal with a white foot. All in all, there were eight cattle that pulled the wagon.

As we moved slowly along, Mama said, 'You know, we are luckier than many of the other families that have had to move. We already have a hut waiting for us at Hukuwa, the one your father and I built when we were first married. At least we won't have to start from the very beginning, even if the hut will need to be fixed.' This did not make me feel better. I had never lived in that place. I had only ever lived on our side of the river.

Our trek ended at sunset that same evening. The day had been long and difficult, and we were all very tired. Mama brought the ox wagon to a standstill and looked at what was left of her old house. The walls were still standing, but the roof had long since vanished. It must have brought back many memories. I wondered if she was thinking about my father, Tata. The man I had never known.

Hearing the wagon approach their home, my aunt and uncle, my father's brother and his wife who lived in the hut a short distance away, came outside to welcome us. They had stayed here for many years, and Mama once told me that they had wanted her to come back and live with them after Tata died.

'Nose!' my uncle beamed as he walked towards Mama with open arms. 'We welcome you all! You finally came home. Your husband would have come back from the grave to strangle me if you would have died away from us.'

I think he meant well, but I did not like him talking like that. About Mama dying. But she did not seem to mind because she was smiling, even though I knew that her smile did not reach her heart. By the lines on her face, I knew that her heart was aching. All Mama wanted was to be back at home, sitting under the old thorn tree.

Then my uncle turned to us children.

'Ntsodo, Ntsodo,' he called. 'Come here, my brother's son. And Mziwakhe, come and shake my hand! Ntsodo tell me, why is your voice sounding like that?' Ntsodo was very hoarse because he had been calling and whistling to the cattle all day long. Despite my misery, I had to laugh. He did sound very strange.

My uncle's name was Jonga and his wife's name was Nomamfengu. They did seem very pleased to have us there. They really tried to make us feel at home, cooking us supper and laughing and joking with us, and I thanked them for that. They said we could stay with them until we had a roof for our new home. There was no rush for us to leave, they told us. As their family, we were more than welcome.

Yes, I remember all these things as if they happened yesterday. But the truth is that they all took place a long time ago. More than forty years. It seems strange to look back so far in time and feel that it was not that long ago. And to see how the course of my life was gently starting to shift, like a river moving a little to the south or north with each flood.

For our move pushed my fate in a new direction. My whole life might have been different if we had not left our home.

Because soon after that day I met my husband.

4

The first time I met Jongile

About a week after we arrived, on a hot and blustery Saturday, Mama and I left our uncle and aunt's home very early to cut thatch at a faraway farm. We needed that thatch to build a roof for our new home.

When Mama woke me, I was still feeling quite sleepy. It was only about half past five in the morning. After a bit of stretching I got dressed and, with eyes still only half open, started to make food for our journey.

Mama Cidi, one of Mama's old friends from when she lived on this side of the river with my father, came with us. She was a very kind lady, about the same age as Mama, but she had lived a very different life. When she was a girl of twenty, she fell pregnant by her boyfriend. From that moment on, her life was filled with worry. She was no longer allowed to go to school or to go to concerts or anything like that.

Her parents told her to marry an old widower, who was about sixty years old, a man old enough to be her grandfather. That was Xhosa tradition. If a girl got pregnant without a husband, she was called *nkazana*. She was not regarded as a lady because she had brought shame to her family. So if there was an elderly man in the community who wanted a wife, he would give her parents lobola and she would have to go to him.

In addition to the child she was pregnant with when they got married, Mama Cidi had three children with that old man, three girls, all of whom she was very close to. I can remember seeing her come past our home, pushing that husband in a wheelbarrow. By that time, he was so old that this was the only way to get him to the shop to collect his old-age pension.

Falling pregnant without a husband brought instant disgrace to a family and ruined a young girl's dreams for the future. The last time I heard of a young unmarried girl getting pregnant was about six years ago, in 1998. My cousin, the same one Grace and I went to see after voting for Mr Mandela, told me that his sixteen-year-old daughter, who lived with her mother in the Eastern Cape close to my own home, had come to the Strand to visit her father. By the end of that holiday, she had got pregnant by some boy. When my cousin found out, he and a few other men took her to that boy's parents.

This boyfriend denied that he was the father of the baby, so the men decided to wait for the baby to be born. Then they would be able to tell by the baby's looks whether he was the father or not. I think that boy must have become very scared, because just before the baby was born he ran away without paying for the damage. My cousin took his daughter and the baby home to his wife in the Eastern Cape.

While he was there, he heard of an old man who had many children already, but as his wife had died, this old man wanted to remarry. So my cousin told his daughter that she must go to him. He gave eight head of cattle for her, and off she went.

I later heard that, some time after going to live with her husband, the girl ran away, back to the Strand. She didn't want to be married to that old man. I don't know where she went, but she was hiding from her father so that he would not force her to go back. I have no idea what happened to that old man. Or to his lobola.

That tradition is still happening, even though today, I think, young women don't stay with those old husbands anymore.

This thatch farm was very far away, in Thrift, but in those days people used to walk for days looking for jobs, so it wasn't unusual for us to walk for most of the day to get thatch. Besides, in the wagon it would have taken three days to get there. Walking allowed us to cut through the fields, which was much quicker.

Our food for the journey was *amasi*, and *umphokoqo,* cooked mealie meal. We carried spoons to pour the sour milk on the *umphokoqo*. It was a very solid meal, good *padkos*. Once we had had our fill, it would take a long time to get hungry again.

We had this meal at about two o'clock in the afternoon, after we had already walked for many hours. We felt quite tired and sat down in the shade of a huge tree to eat our food. Afterwards, Mama and Mama Cidi lay down for a bit to rest, while I went looking for birds' nests.

I loved birds so much I could be with them all day! I didn't think there was anything better than to listen to their song, and to watch them build their homes from leaves and twigs.

We started our journey again a little later, following footpaths across the fields. Some of the walk even took us along very steep cliffs. When the sun became too hot for us, we stopped to cool our hot dry feet in the river that ran along the fields.

Most of the time, I skipped along in front of Mama and Mama Cidi, asking them every now and then, 'Do I have to turn somewhere?' And Mama Cidi would say, 'No, Nomfusi. You just walk straight.' So I'd carry on looking for birds and singing all the while. My song went something like this:

'Yhu! Yhu! Yhu! Solala phi?
Yhu! Yhu! Yhu! Solala phi?
Eli langa liya tshona solala phi.'

This means,

'Ah! Ah! Ah! Where do we sleep?
Ah! Ah! Ah! Where do we sleep?
The sun is setting, where do we sleep?'

After many more hours of walking, Mama Cidi said to Mama, 'Awu, Nose. I don't think we will make it to that farm today!' She peered into the distance and, pointing at a rondavel on top of a hill, said, 'We must go to that house and ask for a place to sleep.'

That is what people used to do in those days. Stopping at a stranger's house, asking for a bed to sleep at night was nothing unusual. If there were no houses nearby, and no shelter to be had, people would just sleep on the side of the road. Every traveller carried water and coffee and sugar and matches, and even a black pot on three legs and mugs and dishes to cook their mealie-meal and coffee. And it would be safe. In those days, we weren't afraid to be robbed or attacked or raped.

But if there was a house close by, it was the custom to ask for a place to sleep.

So we headed towards that rondavel on the hill. When we got there, the sun was already low. Mama Cidi knocked on the door. A man opened the door and, seeing that we were tired, invited us in.

'Oh, visitors!' he said, clapping his hands. 'You are welcome. Have you come from far?'

He seemed a very nice man, and perhaps he felt a bit sorry for us for having walked such a long way. We followed him into his home, and there met his wife, a gentle-looking lady of maybe forty years old. Her eyes lit up when she saw us, and she called out to her daughter. 'Nomvula! Come quickly! Put the mat on the floor for our guests to sit. They look very tired. They have come a long way.'

The daughter also seemed pleased to see us. She was so nice! It was like being welcomed by an old friend. Her face was smiling and her brown eyes were so warm. I think she was about the same age as me. She asked my name and told me hers. I thought Nomvula was a very pretty name for a girl. The meaning of it is 'rain'. Her parents named her that because she was born on a rainy day.

Nomvula put a grass mat on the floor for us to sit on, after which her mother told her to cook us supper. 'Give our guests some stamped cooked mealies,' said her mother. 'And pour some sour milk from the calabash.'

The food was very good and filling, making me feel so tired I could hardly keep my eyes open. Even before this kind family could show us where we could sleep, I had dozed off on Mama's lap, waking only a little when she put me down on the sleeping mat made of rushes, which we call *ukhuko*. I vaguely remember her kissing me goodnight, and then it was dark.

I slept deeply that night and woke before it was dawn. I had been dreaming that I was out in the fields making a wee-wee on the green grass when I woke up. It was still very dark. The first thing I realised was that my dream had been real! I tried to wake Mama, whispering that I made a wee-wee in my sleep, but she was so tired from that long walk that she just slept on. I was so embarrassed!

Luckily, I was sleeping in my panties only, so I took them off and put them in my bag. Even to this day, I don't know why I made a wee-wee in my sleep. Maybe it was because I was not used to sleeping in a strange place.

Once Mama and everyone had woken up, Nomvula gave us nice hot coffee to drink. She also bought us a basin filled with fresh water, so that we could wash. And that's when I had a good idea. Still feeling very ashamed about my accident, I made as if I tripped with that basin of water, spilling it all over that sleeping mat. I felt a bit bad about it, but I was also happy because no one ever found out that I had made a wee-wee there.

The new day was completely different to the night before, when the sky had been clear and the white moon had smiled down on us. Now there was no sun at all, and the sky was grey, like dirty water.

After thanking this kind family, we got ready to go. We still had a very long way to go. Mama Cidi said that the road ahead was even longer than the one we had walked already. So we left, waving back at our new friends as they grew smaller in the distance.

Already we had run out of our *padkos* – I remember wondering if we had eaten too much of it the day before – so by the middle of the morning Mama Cidi said, 'There is a farm about three hours' walk from here. We will stop there and ask for some food for the rest of our journey.'

I felt a little bad about going to a stranger's home again and asking for food, but Mama Cidi said that we had no choice, and that we would do the same for people if they came to our houses.

We arrived at the farm at about lunchtime. Mama Cidi had told us that this farm was owned by a white man who had a lot of labourers working for him. Sure enough, we saw many workers coming in from the fields for lunch. One of these men saw us and offered to take us to the owner.

'Hello, Mama,' he said cheerfully. 'Please come with me before my boss sits down for his lunch. I must take you to him so he knows you are here.'

He knocked at the farmer's kitchen door and was answered by a flood of black and white dogs. They were very friendly, but making lots of noise. I wasn't scared of them. No, they just reminded me of Chuku, making me realise how much I missed him. And missing him made me think of Nori, and how I wished she was there with me.

The farmer came into the kitchen, shushing the dogs, and asked us, in excellent Xhosa, where we had come from. Mama told him that we had come from Hukuwa and that we were on our way to the thatch farm at Thrift, but that we had no more *padkos* for the road.

'Of course,' the white farmer smiled. 'You are welcome to some food.' He turned to the man who had taken us to him and said, 'Please, Vuyo, take these women to your home and give them something to eat. You people have lots of milk from my cows. Give them some *amasi*, and let them rest. They look tired!'

We were happy to hear this, and so we went with the labourer to his home, where his wife gave us a meal. After this, Mama and Mama Cidi had a little nap in the shade of a large tree. I did not sleep, even though I was tired. Instead, I walked around, looking at the fields and listening out for birds.

After their rest, Mama and Mama Cidi thanked the man's wife for giving them *mphokoqo*, crumbed porridge, and *amasi*, and we went on our way again. I did not have *amasi* that day. I ate the *mphokoqo* with boiled water and sugar instead, because by our tradition a young girl my age is not allowed to take milk, except if she is at her own home.

In Xhosa tradition there are many rules about what a girl can and cannot eat. For example, if she is having her monthly time, she cannot take *amasi*, even at her own house, for five days. Only after those days are finished is she allowed to take *amasi* again. We were told that if we drank milk during the time we were bleeding our bodies would need sex. We were also never allowed to eat eggs at any time during the teenage years before marriage. Never.

We walked on for a long time, but even on this second day we had not gone far enough to get to the thatch farm, so we had to look for another place to sleep that evening. Mama Cidi said that we were close to the home of Mr July, which was not very far from the thatch farm, and that she had stayed with this man before. 'He is a very good man,' she told us, and she was sure that he would be happy to give us a place to sleep for the night.

She was right. Mr July and his family welcomed us very warmly. They gave us water to wash and then a tasty supper of samp and green vegetables. Later, I found out that this Mr July was a friend of my future husband's father, but of course I did not know this at the time.

We arrived at the thatch farm the next morning, the third day of our journey. There, we were met by a white farmer, Mr Price.

'*Molo, nkosi!*' we chanted cheerfully, happy that this long journey was finally over.

'*Molweni, nonke.* Good day to you all,' the farmer replied in Xhosa, waving his hand.

I remember being impressed that these white farmers spoke Xhosa so well. Later, when I went to Somerset West, I didn't come across one white person who spoke my language until that day in 1994, when I voted for the first time.

I looked at this man, Mr Price. He was very big, tough and strong looking, with a skin thickened by the sun and a bushy yellow moustache. His thick legs stuck out of his khaki shorts like tree trunks.

'*Ndinganenzela ntoni?*' he asked. 'What can I do for you? *Nivela phi?* Where do you come from?'

'We are coming from Hukuwa and we are here to look for thatch,' Mama explained.

The farmer called to one of the workers behind him. 'Jongile! Show these people to Penelope's home. She and her husband must please give them the keys to the visitors' rondavel.'

I looked at this man, Jongile. He was young, with a very dark skin, a long, straight nose and round, black eyes. Work at the farm made him fit and strong. He looked about twenty-four years old. At the farmer's words, Jongile got off his tractor and, wiping his hands on his blue overall, tipped his khaki hat in greeting.

That was the first time I saw my husband.

He didn't show any interest in me that first time he saw me. But in the two weeks that followed, in which Mama and Mama Cidi cut many bunches of thatch while I cooked for them and kept them company, Jongile gave me a lot of attention.

When we were finished, half the thatch we had cut went to the farmer, and the other half we were allowed to keep. We were finally ready to go home. Jongile and some other men loaded our bunches of thatch onto a truck and Jongile drove us back to Hukuwa. I was relieved that we didn't have to walk again.

All the way home, Jongile was chatting and joking with Mama and Mama Cidi. He was at his most charming, and when he smiled at me, I smiled back.

'Ladies,' he said, a naughty twinkle in his eyes. 'I am a bachelor.' He paused a moment, as if thinking of what to say next. 'There are many, many bachelors at the farm, so the next time your daughter comes to visit us she will not be able to escape so easily.'

Mama's eyebrows shot up. 'No, no, no,' she said, throwing Jongile an angry look. 'Nomfusi will not visit this farm again. She is only sixteen years old, still a schoolgirl. My family and I are looking forward to the day that she becomes a school-teacher!'

I was so happy Mama said that. This good-looking man who seemed so comfortable with himself made me feel very shy. From then until we got home, I ignored him and looked away from him. But, from the corner of my eye, I couldn't help seeing that he was still looking at me. And smiling.

He didn't talk about me anymore, and spoke instead of other things. He told us that he didn't want to work any longer at the thatch farm, that he was applying for a job as an official at the labour department in Queenstown. If he got the position, he would be issuing permits to people who wanted to work in the town. I stayed quiet. I turned my back to him and didn't say another word all the way home.

I could not have known that this man was going to change my life forever.

5

Me on horseback

One morning, about two months later, Mama told me to go to the general dealer in Hukuwa to buy some mealie meal and vegetable oil. She had arranged for me to go with Nomakula, whose mother also needed something from the shop.

It was a Saturday, and although it was March, nearly autumn, and early in the day, it was already very hot. The sun had climbed high in the sky and settled there, beating down on us as we walked along the gravel road. Winter seemed a long way off.

'*Likhupha iintlanzi emanzini!*' I said. This is a Xhosa expression meaning, 'It is so hot that the fish are jumping out of the water!' Nomakula laughed and we started to sing the Malan song.

> '*Iyakunyathel' iAfrika*
> *Malan lumka wanyathelwa*
> *Iyakunyathel' iAfrika*
> *Malan lumka wanyathelwa*
> *Malan lumka wanyathelwa!*'

As always, the best part was the chorus. Here our voices rose, and the wind carried those proud words away. '*Afrika! Afrika! Afrika!*' And again, this time louder. '*Afrika! Afrika! Afrika!*' And then we laughed with the happiness of it all.

Just as we were starting to sing this song again, we heard the muffled sound of a horse galloping behind us on the road. We moved aside to let the rider pass. Imagine our surprise when, instead of thundering ahead, the horse stopped next to us on that gravel road. My surprise grew even more when I saw who the rider was. Jongile from the thatch farm! That handsome man with those naughty eyes and a smile that made me blush.

All the shyness I had felt the time he drove Mama, Mama Cidi and me home came flooding back. I tried to hide my feelings by lowering the straw hat I was wearing against the sun.

Jongile touched his finger to his forehead in greeting and made his wide-chested horse rear up in front of us. He was showing off, of course, but I could not blame him. His horse was very beautiful. It had a reddish-brown colour and a white star on its forehead.

Jongile also looked very handsome, and a flutter rose from the bottom of my stomach at seeing him there. Even though I didn't realise it then, he had already come to mean something to me.

'*Tyhini!* My goodness! What are you doing here, *bhuti*?' I asked.

We Xhosa people call men and women a little older than ourselves *bhuti* or *sisi*, meaning 'brother' or 'sister'. In the same way, we call older men *tata*, meaning father, and older women *mama*, meaning mother. As a sign of respect.

I hadn't seen Jongile since he dropped us off from collecting thatch, but he hadn't changed much. He was wearing grey trousers and a checked shirt, and his dark brown eyes were shining like those of a schoolboy full of mischief.

'*Molo*, Nomfusi,' he said, grinning. 'What am I doing here? Well, ladies, when I see a beautiful flower I make it a habit to stop and look at it.'

Awu! That man! He was flirting again.

'My dear friend,' I said to Nomakula. 'This brother's name is Jongile. He stays near the Nkonkobe Mountains.' Then I turned to Jongile, who was still sitting on his beautiful horse. 'Bhuti, this is Nomakula. We are best friends and are in the same class at school.'

Jongile turned to my friend and bowed. 'Hello, princess. I am very pleased to meet you. What beauties I am finding here in front of me today!'

Yes, that was typical of Jongile. He was a very charming man.

He offered Nomakula his hand, which she took, and helped her onto his horse. I knew she would find Jongile very attractive. She giggled when he told her the horse's name was Kombuis, and said yes when he offered to take her for a ride. Kombuis neighed and bucked a bit, making me feel nervous.

Jongile then dug his heels into the horse, and together he and Nomakula galloped off, leaving me and my uncertain thoughts alone on that gravel road. When they came back a few minutes later, Nomakula's eyes shone with excitement.

'How about you, Nomfusi?' Jongile teased. He jumped off Kombuis's back and, dust flying all around us, helped Nomakula down. 'Or are you too afraid to get on my big horse?'

Well, I was a bit scared, but I was not going to allow this man to laugh at me! So I stuck out my chin and said, 'I am not afraid of your horse, Bhuti. I will gladly get on his back with you.'

Thinking back, I should have known that this was what he had wanted all along. But I was no more than a schoolgirl. How could I have known?

He jumped back on his horse and held out his hand. I took it and he lifted me easily up behind him. Over the noise of Kombuis's hooves and my own excited breathing, I could not hear my destiny changing.

For after that moment, my life would never be the same again.

6

Longing to go home

I think Nomakula realised even before me what was going on.
I can still hear her voice, shouting my name, crying after me.
She knew what was happening. This was *thwala*, the Xhosa
custom for taking a bride.

Thwala is a very old tradition, and it still happens in some
places today. But this is seldom. Today, especially in the big
towns and cities, young girls choose their own husbands. But
then, in those days, this is what happened to us young girls.

The tradition says that if a man wants a girl to be his bride,
he first speaks to the girl's parents, offering lobola for her. If the
parents like the man and he can offer a lot of cattle for her, the
more happy the parents will be for their daughter to marry him.
Once they have made a deal, the man can then take this girl
away with him to his home. From that time on, she is his young
wife. His *makoti*.

But the girl knows nothing about all this. On the day that
she is taken, the parents will send her on an errand – maybe to
fetch firewood for cooking, or to bring fresh water from the
river. This is to get her out of the house and to an agreed place
where her future husband will be waiting to grab her.

According to tradition, the husband-to-be is supposed to
bring a few other men along, and it is they who actually take
her. The husband does not touch her until she is in his house.

You can imagine the shock this girl gets! But if she sees that her boyfriend is among these men who grab her, she will be happy because she will know that she is to be the wife of the man she loves.

Sometimes she will be taken by a stranger she has never met, a man who has been watching her for a long time and has spoken to her parents without her knowing him. And sometimes the man who has been watching the girl he wants to marry like a hawk will take her to his home *before* asking permission from the girl's parents and offering to pay them lobola. But this is not really tradition, and it does not normally happen.

Most of these marriages do work out. The couple have many children together and the woman stays with her husband until she or he dies.

Once, when I was a young girl, I heard *thwala* happening. I was visiting my aunt at her home with my older sister, Thwenya. We had gone into the fields, leaving behind the houses that were near some big stone cliffs. That place was very beautiful.

Suddenly we heard a loud cry from a girl and some men singing. I asked my sister what was going on, but then I heard that girl crying and I knew. As a child I had grown up hearing about these old traditions and so I knew that with *thwala*, the girl who is taken has to cry. That is the custom. She is not supposed to keep quiet, even if she loves that man who is taking her to his home.

She cries to show that she is sad and scared to leave her home and parents. And the men like it when she cries. If she doesn't, they think that she will try to run away when she gets a chance.

It was only later on that I found out that one of those men who had taken part in the *thwala* that day was the son of my aunt. It was he who took the girl. And she never tried to run away from him. No, she loved him, and stayed with him for the rest of her life, giving him many children.

Kombuis was going very fast, making me feel quite scared. We were flying along that gravel road, kicking up a cloud of fine dust as we sped along. I remember thinking that Jongile was showing off the strength of his horse, but, when after some time he still hadn't stopped, I realised what was going on.

This man is not playing a game with me. We were not going back to Nomakula, and I was not going back home. Oh, dear Lord, I would never be a schoolgirl again. I was going to be a married lady, with long dresses and no education.

And no Mama.

There was nothing I could do. Nothing but hold on to this young man who was taking me away from everything I knew to make me his wife.

After what felt like hours, Jongile made his horse slow down and turned around to look at me. I think he began to feel a bit sorry for me, because he saw I was very confused and unhappy.

'Don't worry, Nomfusi,' he said gently. 'As your husband, I will make you happy. We will be very happy together.'

But no kind words could take away the soreness in my heart. I was crying all the way there.

'Please, Bhuti,' I begged him. 'I can't live without Mama and my school.' But Jongile did not answer.

When I realised that he was not going to give in, I told myself that if I couldn't do anything to change things right then, on that horse, maybe once we got to his home everything would be sorted out. I would tell him that I did not want to be married and that I wanted to finish school. Then he would understand and take me back.

About a kilometre before his home, Jongile reined in Kombuis and got off, helping me down also. I don't remember what the time was but I remember that I could not see much of what was around me, it was already too dark to see anything. I wondered why we were stopping.

I soon found out.

Jongile took my face and turned it towards his. He was

standing very close to me. Then he said, 'My wife, please kiss me! I love you so, so much. You know why you are here, don't you? I am going to lobola my cattle to your parents for you. And you will be my wife from now on.'

I did not know what to do, because I realised that I *did* like this man. He was very attractive and already I felt comfortable with him. But I didn't want to be married yet. I wanted to finish school. So I thought, I had better do what he says. Maybe, if I give him his kiss, maybe then he won't think I will run away when he takes me to his home.

So I did. I kissed him.

I did not like it and was not wanting to do it again soon. But it looked as if Jongile did enjoy it, so I thought I should take my chance. 'Ag, Jongile. If you love me so much, then why don't you wait until I have finished my education for me to marry you?' I asked him. 'I still have some time to go in school. I want to be a teacher.'

But he shook his head. 'I am sorry, Nomfusi, I do not want to wait until that time.' He was silent for a moment, and I shivered. The sun had set and it was very dark and cold. I don't know what Jongile's thoughts were as he helped me back onto his horse and we rode the last bit to his home, which I later found out was about ten kilometres along the same road as that thatch farm where Mama, Mama Cidi and I had first met him.

When we arrived, paraffin lamps shone dimly from inside three huts. One of them belonged to Jongile, and the other two were his parents'. These were the last rondavels before the Nkonkobe Mountains, a beautiful place that is full of snow in winter. They are called Winterberge. The winter mountains.

On hearing the horse, a small dog that was lying in front of the main rondavel got up and started barking. When it heard Jongile's voice it stopped. It was now so cold that I was shivering even under the thick jacket Jongile had given me after our kiss. The cold autumn night came right through it.

'Come, Nomfusi.'

Jongile opened the door to one of the smaller rondavels and, while he lit one of the paraffin lamps on a wooden table, I looked around the room. There was only one bed, the table with the lamp, and a wooden stool.

Jongile watched me looking at everything. 'Relax, Nomfusi,' he said, not unkindly. 'I will go and ask my sisters to fetch some wood to make a fire for you so that you can wash yourself. Then you will be warm.'

I nodded gratefully. Maybe I will feel better when I am warm, I tried to convince myself.

'I will be right back,' Jongile said, one hand on the doorknob. 'I will tell my parents that you are here. I had already told them that I was going to see you at your home, and that I wanted to choose a woman myself. Not someone they chose for me.'

And with that, he left. A gust of freezing night air swept through the room before he closed the door behind him. It was a menacing sort of cold and I shivered again. From the cold, and from my fear.

Of course, I had no clothes or things with me to prepare for a night away from home. No towel or even a change of underwear. Not even a toothbrush. Well, I didn't really worry much about a toothbrush. In those days, we did not have the money to buy the Colgates and the toothbrushes in shops. We just used wood ash and our fingers to clean our teeth at night.

For a while I was still, just standing there, thinking my own private thoughts. A few minutes later, there was a knock on the door. It was Nontombi and Boniwe, Jongile's younger sisters. Their names, of course, I did not know at that moment, only later on. Like I also learnt that there were four sisters and four brothers in their family.

These two sisters were very friendly to me. They were smiling and saying, 'Hello, Nomfusi! You are welcome!'

Each sister carried a big pile of wood into the rondavel, which they put on the floor and started building the fire. While they were busy, I looked at them. Jongile's siblings.

They, like their brother, were very striking. Nontombi shared her brother's coffee bean-coloured skin, while Boniwe was lighter than them both.

There was a crackle as the kindling took flame. Soon the fire was going well. Orange flames were licking the heavy pieces of wood, slowly heating up the chilly room. The fire gave off a lot of thick smoke, making it difficult for me to breathe, but the windows were open so it could escape from there. That was the tradition. A fire was made inside the hut, its smoke only able to leave through the window. At home, we also had fires inside the house to cook with and to warm us in winter, but we used dry wood from a tree called *umnga*. That is the mimosa tree, I think. Their wood was different, and it made my eyes sore.

Jongile returned a little while later and, satisfied that the fire was going well, asked Nontombi and Boniwe to bring me blankets and some leftover food. The family had already had their supper, but I of course hadn't eaten anything since that morning. Not that I was hungry. Up to that moment, I hadn't even thought about food.

Jongile watched his sisters leave in silence, then told me that he would sleep in the other rondavel. I would have the room, and the fire, to myself.

I was very happy to hear that.

'Tomorrow, I will bring my parents to meet my *makoti*, my new wife,' said Jongile breezily before he closed the door behind him.

And then I was alone.

I did not want to be there! I wanted to go home. *Please*, I thought. *I want to be with Mama.*

A few minutes later, Nontombi reappeared with some cooked samp and hot tea to drink. I was not allowed to drink sour milk now, as a newlywed woman is not allowed to take this at the house of her in-laws. Only much later, when a bride has been living with her in-laws for several years, may she take *amasi* again. That is tradition.

I didn't sleep at all well that night. I was restless, dreaming all sorts of strange things, leaving me tired and slow the next morning. Shortly after I woke up I was introduced to my mother-in-law, who I was to call Ma. She saw that I felt very unhappy and she tried to make me feel at ease by welcoming me into her family.

Ma's skin was very dark, almost pitch black. Yes, I could see where Jongile and his sister Nontombi got their good looks. She was a very handsome woman indeed.

My father-in-law did not come to see me. Xhosa custom said that he could only see me once I was dressed in the long skirts and dresses that married ladies wear. There were also other rules to follow, now that I was a newly married woman. For example, I was not allowed to leave the rondavel until my father-in-law went to see my mother to arrange lobola. Until a deal had been made, I was not allowed to go anywhere and had to stay in the hut all day long.

Also, I was never left by myself. If Nontombi was not with me inside the hut, her younger sister, Boniwe, was. If I had to go to the toilet, one of them would come with me. We used to go to the toilet in the bushes, but even then I was not allowed to be alone. Never, never, never!

I spoke with Nontombi a lot, and it was she who told me about her family. Apparently, the eldest of my husband's four sisters was in George, training as a witchdoctor. She came home several years later after my marriage to Jongile. By that time, I had already given birth to Bukelwa, my third daughter, of whom she was very fond. Her name was Nomsa, and she loved me and my children very much. She died a few years later after a short illness. After she passed away, her parents raised her only son.

After Nomsa there was Nokhaya, Nontombi and Boniwe. There were also four brothers, with Jongile the oldest son. His brothers and sisters are all still living in Queenstown. I go there to visit them when I go back on holiday. Even now, in 2004.

Those first days at my new home were a blur. I remember Jongile going back Queenstown in his car. He would be back at the weekend.

Before he left, he told me that he had been married before, but that his wife had left him. That he had another wife before that one, he didn't say. Jongile kept on saying that I was the only wife for him, but I never answered. I was too busy thinking of a way to run back home.

To Mama.

I stayed in that rondavel for a whole week, sitting there by myself and doing nothing. It is customary for a new bride to work for her in-laws, doing all sorts of things like cooking, cleaning and fetching water from the river, but as my family had not yet come to an agreement with Jongile's parents, I wasn't officially his wife yet. They couldn't make me work, and I had nothing to do.

One evening, shortly after my arrival, I was bathing in my hut when Nontombi said, 'Nomfusi, you have beautiful smooth arms. They remind me of my brother's first wife! She also had a very light skin, like you.'

I asked her where this first wife was.

'Awu! My brother did not tell you about his wife?'

'Yes, he did,' I said to her. After all, he did tell me about his wife.

But then my sister-in-law said something I did not know. 'She had two children by my brother and took them away with her after my brother told her that he didn't want her anymore,' Nontombi told me. 'They were fighting and fighting, and when my brother left for work one day this woman took all her clothes and her children and left. She never came back!'

Children? I knew nothing about children! I felt so shocked. My body began to tremble but, not wanting her to see that I was upset, I asked her to tell me everything there was to tell about that brother of hers.

She said, '*Awu! Nceda, sisi!* Don't tell my family that I told you!'

I told her that I would not, but that I did want to know why Jongile had chased his wife away.

'This first wife of my brother, she was caught by my mother stealing sugar and mealies that she gave to her parents.'

'Did Jongile see that for himself?'

'No.'

'Then how can your brother believe in something he did not see for himself?' I thought this all sounded very strange and I was starting to feel very uneasy. Then she told me about the second wife.

'After the first wife went away, my parents asked my brother to take another girl, one that they liked very much. She came to the house with my sister, Nokhaya, who brought her there without telling her. They never let her go. When my brother came home from work to find this girl at his home, he was told that she was to be his wife.'

Jongile's father then took his horse and rode to that girl's parents, where they spoke about lobola. But then, when Jongile met me at the thatch farm, he changed his mind, telling his parents that she must go.

The third wife, then, was me.

For the second time since I had been taken by Jongile, I couldn't sleep with worry. Already then, in those very early days, Jongile had been untruthful with me. I didn't know anything about a second wife, and crying, I had only one thought on my mind. *How am I going to get away from here? I must find a way to go home.*

The next day, my father-in-law and a friend – who I saw through the window of the rondavel was Mr July, the same man Mama, Mama Cidi and I had stayed with that one night – saddled up their horses. My father-in-law told Ma that he was going to visit my family to tell them that his son had taken me for his wife. As they rode away, I thought to myself, *You can go, but it won't be long before I will sneak away. And then I will be gone from this place.*

It was a long day, and the waiting was terrible, but at last, around midnight, my father-in-law and Mr July came home. I had tried to stay up until I heard their horses, but was so tired that I had fallen asleep. The sound of the dog barking, however, woke me up, and when I heard the galloping horses I knew that they had come home. Home from my home. Home from Mama.

The next morning, I was told that Mama and my uncle had agreed for me to be Jongile's wife but, since lobola had not been paid, my new husband was not yet allowed to touch me.

When Jongile came home from work the next weekend, he was very happy to see me and proudly showed me the material he had brought for me from Queenstown. This material was for the new clothes that I had to wear as a *makoti*, a young bride. My mother-in-law was going to make these new clothes for me with her sewing machine.

Then Jongile said, 'My mother is giving you a new name, Nomfusi. You will be called Nowam.' That is the custom, for a new wife to be given a new name. This is to respect her. If her parents-in-law call her by her maiden name, it means they don't want her. It is an insult for a woman's in-laws to call her by her maiden name.

Jongile went back to Queenstown that same night. But before he left, he told me that he was coming home soon for a holiday. To be with me. I did not say anything to him, but I was thinking to myself. *By the time you come home, Jongile, I will be long gone. Back home, and wearing my own clothes.*

My mother-in-law made me a very long skirt with the material that Jongile brought from Queenstown. It was so long that you could not even see my ankles. The colour was blue with a white print. There was also a petticoat, which was of a very thick and warm material. The blouse was long-sleeved and there was also a pair of new black walking shoes. Over all this

I had to wear a blanket that was wrapped around me under-neath my arms and fastened by a safety pin over my shoulder.

Then lastly there was the *doek*, or *iqhiya*, a black scarf that was wrapped tightly around my head. It went down so low over my forehead that I could only see my feet. If I wanted to see anything else I had to tilt my head up to the sky and glance out from under this *doek*.

This was also part of Xhosa tradition. The new *makoti* has to show respect for her parents-in-law, and it is not allowed for her to look them straight in the eye. Only after many years of marriage does this *doek* go higher onto her head, until eventu-ally it looks like a turban. So a woman who has known marriage for many years may wear a very high *iqhiya*. This looks very beautiful.

I was made to work from the very first day that I was wearing these new clothes. The family took away those clothes I was wearing from my home. I don't know what they did with them. It was like they threw away part of me.

Then my mother-in-law said, 'You put on these new clothes, and then you can start doing housework. From this day, you must wake up at six o'clock in the morning and make us coffee and roast *koek*.'

So from then on I got up very early each morning to make breakfast for everybody. Roast *koek*, and *amasi*, too. Roast *koek* is a type of bread that is made by kneading flour and leaving it to rise. When it is ready, the dough is rolled out and cut into nice pieces and then it is roasted over wood coals. It is very tasty.

Jongile's family had lots of milk from their cows for *amasi*, and even had a machine that they used to turn the milk into butter. I had only seen a machine like that before on the white man's farm where Nomi and her husband worked.

Then, one Saturday, Nontombi told me that there was going to be a party the next day. I knew that everybody would be busy organising this party. They would be too busy and excited to watch over me.

And that was when I had the idea.

On the morning of the party, I got up even earlier than normal to do my chores. I made breakfast, and as usual it was *mphokoqo* with sour milk. It was my father-in-law's favourite breakfast.

After they had finished their meal, my parents-in-law left to go to church on a neighbouring farm, by which time I had finished cooking the heavy mealie bread. This bread is made by grinding dried mealies on a flat stone, after which they are soaked overnight before being made into a very solid bread that can be eaten with sour milk and tea or coffee.

By this time, the first guests had started to arrive. Soon the boys and girls were dancing, and laughing and drinking *umqombothi*, the traditional African beer that is also made from mealies. They were all enjoying themselves so much that no one was paying attention to me. Not even Nontombi.

That was my chance! I slipped around the back of one of the three rondavels, where I knew the boys who had come to the party had left their bicycles, thinking that I would be able to take one and get away unseen.

Bicycles are a wonderful thing. I had learnt to ride a bike the year before, when I visited my sister Ntemntem and her husband at their home. There were always lots of boys with bikes around who liked to flirt with the girls and were happy to teach a fifteen-year-old girl how to ride.

And now one of these was going to save me from being kept at Jongile's home.

I grabbed the best-looking one, and also a pump, and pushed that bike as silently as I could through the long grass until I reached the gravel road. It was exactly the middle of the day. Then I took deep breath and looked around one last time to make sure that no one was watching me. I reached down to pull up that hateful long skirt and tuck it inside the elastic of my panties before I got onto that bike. It did not matter that it was a man's bike. I was used to those.

Without looking back again, I swung my right leg over the bar and put my foot on the pedal. First a little awkward with those clothes, but soon I was going very fast. I pumped my legs like someone trying to get away from a wild animal, racing down the gravel road, making little rocks shoot from underneath the wheels.

I was riding like the wind. Towards my home. To Mama. And no one could stop me.

7

Me on a bicycle

I was going down that gravel road so fast that I almost scared myself. Soon I had reached the home of my father-in-law's friend, Tata July. This was, of course, the same man who had gone to visit Mama with Jongile's father to discuss my lobola. I was quite scared to pass by in case he saw me there, but as there was no other road to take, I had no choice.

Unfortunately for me, Tata July was working close to the road. When I saw him there, I didn't know what I could do other than to greet him. So I got down from that bicycle and, quickly pulling my long dress down to my ankles again, said hello. He looked very surprised to see me there, getting down from that bike. And then came the question I was dreading.

'*Molo*, Nomfusi! Where are you going?'

I didn't answer him right away, because I had no idea what to say. My father-in-law's friend! He *knew* that I was running away, anyone could see that! I felt like a child who is caught doing something naughty. It was a very uncomfortable moment.

'You must go back,' Tata July finally said to me. His voice held no anger at all.

'*Nceda*, Tata,' I said. 'Please, Tata. Let me go home! I do not like it there and I don't want to be married yet. I want to finish my schooling and become a schoolteacher.'

He looked at me for a few moments. Quietly, as if he was making up his mind what to do. I think he wished that he hadn't seen me going past. I felt bad about that, because now this man had to make a difficult decision because of me. But more than that, I felt desperate to go home.

To my surprise, he said, '*Kulungile, ntombam*. All right, my girl. I am going to let you go. But you must never tell anyone that I saw you here today, running away. If your father-in-law knew I let you pass by, he would ask me why I did not send you back. I could be in a lot of trouble.'

I couldn't believe that he was going to let me carry on home. I felt so happy, I could have given him a hug!

'*Awu! Nkosi, yam enkosi, Tata July*,' I said. 'Oh, my Lord! Thank you, Tata.'

As I said before, we black people always called men old enough to be our fathers *tata*. That is Xhosa tradition. The same is with women. I could not say 'Cidi' to my mother's friend. I called her Mama Cidi. That is the way to respect a man or a woman who is not your relative and is older. It is still like that today.

In Xhosa tradition, I cannot even call my own husband by his own name. That would not be respectful. I had to call him by the name of his youngest sister, or if there is no younger sister, by the name of his youngest brother. For example, my mother-in-law told me to call Jongile after his sister, Nontombi. So I must address my husband as *bhuti kaNontombi*, which means Nontombi's brother.

And the husband cannot call his wife by her name either. That's why I was given a new name by my mother-in-law that, from that moment on, everyone in my new family used. I had to call my husband's sisters *sisi omncinci* or *sisi omkhulu*. Younger sister, older sister. The same was with his brothers.

So anyway, I took that bicycle and pushed it along the road until I could no longer see Tata July standing there. The reason I was walking beside it instead of riding it was because as a young woman I had to respect him, and it would be disrespectful to get onto the bike in front of him.

When I arrived at the first farm where Mama, Mama Cidi and I had stayed the night on our way to the thatch farm, I stopped to ask for some water to drink. I had been cycling for quite a long time, and I was very thirsty.

'*Molo! Uphilile?*' the same man who had given us food and shelter that time greeted me this day too. I heard later that he was a distant relative of my family.

'*Molo, Tata. Ndisaphila.* I am alive.'

'How come you are so thirsty? When it's so cold with snow on the mountains?' Then he looked at the bike. 'Whose bike is that? Are you running away?'

He then asked me into his home for some tea or coffee and something to eat, but I did not want to stay.

'No, thank you,' I replied. 'I don't drink tea or coffee, and I am not hungry. I have some roast *koek* with me and just want a bit of water before I carry on.'

I wanted to go now. I was getting nervous that those boys at Jongile's home had noticed that a bike had gone missing.

Again, this man at the house said, 'Whose bike is this?'

I answered him truthfully.

Then, to my surprise, he said, 'You must hurry, Nomfusi. I know Jongile very well, and I think you are too young to be married to him. I know he had two wives already. If those boys come here I will not tell them that I saw you here. Now go, before it gets too dark.'

I was also worried about the dark so, thanking him, I quickly pushed the bicycle to the top of the hill. There, I was out of sight, so I climbed back on the bicycle and carried on my way.

Cycling was so wonderful! That bicycle, I will never forget it. It was perfect! I even forgot that it was not my own. It was wonderful to feel the wind brush against my face. My sorrow at being taken by a man with two previous wives, and what my family might say when they saw me arrive back home, all of that was forgotten. As I went along so fast, the Malan song went through my head. '*Afrika! Afrika! Afrika!*'

Too soon, it started getting cold. The wind grew teeth that bit at my hands, so I took off my *doek* and covered my fingers with it, using it like a glove. Shortly after that, I got off the bicycle to walk past a few herdboys who were sitting around a fire next to the road. They stopped me and asked if I wanted to warm my hands by their fire, but I told them that they were not cold. I didn't want any more stops.

But they were friendly, and I knew they meant well. They could see by my dress that I was a *makoti*, so they didn't bother me. Inwardly, I smiled at that. It seemed that this long dress was good for something after all!

By the time I finally arrived at my uncle's home it was already very dark. I knocked on the door, and a few moments later my cousin opened for me. Surprise was all over his face, but he did not say anything. Instead, he walked with me to Mama's house and, when he got there, he saw me in before turning back.

There was Mama. And I was home.

8

Arriving home again for the first time

Mama let out a cry of joy when she saw me. '*Awu, Nomfusi*! *Mntwana wam!* Oh, Nomfusi! I am so glad you are here!'

She hugged me tightly to her breast before pulling me inside, where the cold night air could not chill us through to our bones. Then she looked at me. I don't think she believed that I was really there. And me, too, I didn't know what to do. Laugh or cry! I was so happy to be home and to see Mama standing beside me. I almost giggled at her shock.

'Sit, sit, sit!' Mama said. 'My poor child, you must be so cold and hungry and tired. Tell me! What happened? Why do you have to come that long way by yourself? Why did you not write me a letter to come and fetch you? Whose bicycle is this? When did you leave?'

And so many other questions. I didn't know where to begin, but before I could open my mouth she was hugging me again. 'Never mind, my child. Shush now. We will talk tomorrow.' Her smile was warm. 'Now you must rest after your long and tiring journey.'

'*Kulungile*, Mama. All right.'

She put more wood on the fire, and together with Mziwakhe, fetched her huge three-legged black pot and filled it with water. Then they carried in the big metal tub that we used for washing clothes and also for bathing.

'When the water is hot, my child,' she said, 'you must take your bath and then go straight under my blankets. I have already made my sleeping place.'

It was the best thing she could have said to me. 'Thank you, Mama. I have missed your blankets and your warmth.'

I had a soothing bath, after which Mama cooked me supper. It never tasted so good! It was a delicious soup with peas and vegetables, which I ate with steamed bread. The best meal I have ever eaten in my life.

Then she told me to rest. Mziwakhe helped her with the dishes. After all that was done, we all lay awake. It was unbelievable, and somehow I couldn't sleep. So I began to tell them of all the things that had happened at my parents-in-law.

I didn't say parents-in-law then, of course, because they were not yet my parents-in-law. I did not have a clue that I would end up marrying Jongile anyway.

Mama said that my uncle was going to come the next day to talk to me, and that I must sleep now and save my stories for tomorrow. I said, 'Yes, Mama. But did you know that Jongile has already had two wives?'

She did not know about that, and she was very shocked to hear the news. Then she said: 'Oh, *nceda,* Ntondo! Go to sleep now. We will talk tomorrow. I am going to give you some hot milk to make you sleep. Don't worry. You are not going back there anymore. You are going back to school.'

I was so glad to hear this that I stopped thinking about Jongile. I drank my warm milk and fell asleep soon after.

The following morning I woke to the sound of soft voices. As I listened, I realised that they belonged to my uncle and his younger brother, Gwebityala. This was his last surviving brother.

I quickly dressed and, when I joined them, my uncle asked if I loved Jongile. 'No, Uncle Jonga. Not at all!' I said with all the strength in my chest. 'I hate him. He has chased away two wives already!'

'What do you mean, Nomfusi? We know from Jongile's father that he and his wife had chosen a woman for him. But we heard that it had not worked out. He told us this when he came to tell us that you were at their home. He told us that since that wife left, Jongile has only worked in Queenstown and has not come back home. He also told us that Jongile is only interested in marrying one wife, and that is you!'

I looked both my uncles straight in the eye and also Mama, who had come to stand beside me. I told them what Nontombi had told me that day in the rondavel.

'Bhuti Jonga,' Mama said. 'My daughter is very young. She wants to go back to school here in Hukuwa.'

'Nose, you know that we have already come to an agreement with Jongile's father on lobola,' said my uncle.

'Yes, Bhuti. This is true. But Nomfusi really wants to become a teacher. And I would like to let her.'

My uncle looked at Mama with tenderness. 'You are a very loving mother, Nose. But you see the trouble in this country. Jongile is a decent man. He has a reliable job. He will work hard to look after your daughter, and any children she may give him. You know he will.'

Mama sighed deeply. 'You may be right, Bhuti. He is a good man.' She put a hand on each of my shoulders and looked me deep in the eye. 'And you know, Nomfusi, I do believe that Jongile loves you.'

'Please, Mama,' I begged her. 'Please! I want to go back to school. I want to be a teacher, or maybe a social worker. I don't want to be married yet!'

But my uncle and Mama stood firm. The following day, both my uncle's wives came to my home, together with one daughter-in-law each, telling Mama that they wanted to speak to me.

That was the way.

'Did he ask you for a kiss?' they asked.

I said yes.

'So did this man kiss you?'

I told them yes again.

Then they asked me if I was still a virgin.

'Yes.'

If Jongile had taken me to his bed without permission from Mama and my uncle, the lobola would have gone up and Jongile would have had to pay eleven cattle instead of ten.

So they were quite satisfied with my answers.

But I was not. I had lost my chance to go back to school. I did not know what kind of future lay ahead of me now.

9

Lobola

Jongile and his father arrived at my home two days later in Jongile's motorcar. They asked to see me, but my uncle told them that they first had to bring the lobola.

Jongile then went to speak to my sister Nomi, who had arrived for a short visit just that day and was cooking some stew for the guests. After he had spoken to her, she told me that he had just about begged her to tell me to run away with him.

But Nomi had refused. 'No. Leave my sister alone,' she had told him. 'She is going back to school. I do not want you to drop my sister like you did those other wives!'

I didn't see Jongile that day. Before they drove off, Jongile told Nomi to ask me to escort him and his father to his car when they left, but I didn't want to. So they left.

I didn't want to think about what would happen next. I knew that Mama and my uncle had again agreed to the marriage, but I put that out of my mind. I tried to forget about Jongile and the arrangement that had been made about my future.

Over the next few months, Jongile sent me many letters, none of which I bothered to answer. I didn't know it at the time, but he also wrote to my mother, sending her packages with food and pieces of material.

I had other things on my mind. My cousin, who was living in Queenstown, had suggested that I attend the Standard Seven school term there. Mama seemed to think that it was a good idea. But before I could go, a letter arrived from Jongile telling Mama that his father was coming to visit my home. He would be bringing the first part of my lobola.

It was a beautiful morning when Jongile's father came, bright and shiny, a perfect spring day. It was also the last day of my innocence. Because that day, that September day, I saw the last of my hopes and dreams.

It started with the sound of my aunts ululating with happiness. They were chanting, 'Welcome to the Majola family.'

'Quickly, Nomfusi,' Mama said. 'Go inside the house. Here comes Jongile's father and Tata July!'

I hurried in, feeling quite scared. Was this man ever going to give up? I had thought it was all over. I was Nomfusi again, wearing my own clothes and staying at my home with Mama. The only home I ever wanted to know.

They had come on horses. And they were herding three young cows in front of them. My relatives appeared out of nowhere, uncles and aunts with their daughters and sons. There was more ululating. The younger boys opened the gates to the kraal in front of the house to let in the cows, and when the gate closed behind them there was still more singing. The guests were given *umqombothi*, African beer.

It is difficult to describe how I felt. Dazed. Confused. Very surprised, and more than a little shocked. *Is this really going to happen? How will I cope without Mama? How will I cope being away from home?*

Later, once everybody had gone, some of my friends and relatives asked me how I could marry a man who had already rejected two wives. They told me to run away from home before Jongile could claim me. But others congratulated me. So many things were going through my mind, and all these people telling me different things made me even more confused. I just couldn't make sense of it all.

'I don't *want* to be married,' I blurted. 'I don't want to be married to *any* man just yet! And I could never run away from my mother!'

That evening, Mama and Uncle Jonga sat me down. Both looked very happy. By this time, Mama was very fond of Jongile, and she couldn't think of a better husband for me than this dashing young man.

'My child,' said Uncle Jonga. 'This is the start. Part of the lobola has been paid for you. There are seven more cattle to come, so you must prepare yourself to be married.'

Nomi was also there, but she was not happy for me to marry this man at all. She said she thought that a man like that would always throw out his wife after having enough of her before taking another one. But Mama and my uncle disagreed with her, saying that those women were not meant for Jongile and that I would stay with Jongile for good.

There was nothing Nomi could say to change their minds. And neither could I.

A few days later, Jongile came to visit us at our home again. This time, he was welcomed with open arms. He stayed all afternoon and all evening, and after supper Nomi and I made a bed for him in one of Mama's other huts, where my brothers used to sleep when they were visiting.

When I showed him his sleeping place, Jongile told me that he wanted to talk to me. 'Nomfusi, I think I must be dreaming. Now you will finally be my wife. My one true wife that I have wanted for such a long time. I am going to work very hard to make the lobola as soon as I can.' He looked at me intently. 'I want you, Nomfusi.'

I didn't know what to say to him, so I just kept quiet. His eyes spoke of things that I knew nothing about. It scared me, but I knew it was too late. Whatever Jongile wanted to do to me as my husband, it would not be long before he could.

The following morning, I woke earlier than usual to make coffee for Jongile as he had to get back to his job in Queenstown that morning. Mama was still asleep, so I silently crept out from underneath our blankets. I was still sleeping with her in her bed.

I didn't think anything would happen then. Why should I have expected anything to happen?

After coffee, I went with Jongile to his car to see him off. But instead of me standing there as he drove away, Jongile grabbed my arm, pushing me across the driver's seat into the passenger seat. He then quickly jumped behind the wheel and, before I knew what was happening, started the car and drove off.

This man was taking me away from my home again! How could this be happening?

Jongile had lied to me. He didn't go to work that day. He took me to his home, jumping out to tell his parents that I was there as soon as we stopped.

It was impossible to tell what Ma thought of me being there. Her eyes and face did not show any feeling. She just gave me one of her own long dresses to wear instead of my own, even though her dresses were much too big for me. She told me that it would only be for a day or so. She said she still had material left from the last time she had made me dresses and that she would use this to make me new ones.

I was also given another *doek* to wear. My mother-in-law tied it tightly around my forehead, but not so tight that it gave me a headache. In our tradition, the new *makoti* doesn't dress herself. Instead, it is the mother-in-law, aunt or sister-in-law who puts on her clothes. It is the way for them to show her how to dress in their home. I was very upset, and cried for my lost freedom.

After my mother-in-law had finished dressing me, she asked me to go to the main rondavel to help Nontombi to stamp the mealies. This was my parents-in-law's main living, dining and sleeping place.

Supper that night was stiff pap and the meat of a sheep that my father-in-law had found dead in the field. It had already been pecked at by the vultures. There were also some wild greens. We ate together while sitting on the floor. We never ate from the table, except on special occasions.

After supper, Jongile went to his room, but I stayed behind in the main rondavel to wash the dishes and sweep the floor. I did this without being asked. I had been taught by Mama to always help, no matter where I was, even when I was visiting my sister or other relatives. I also knew that, as a daughter-in-law, you have to do all the work. My mother-in-law never cooked or washed any dishes or clothes. The same applied to a sister-in-law, unless she wanted to help. Like Nontombi. The only chore my mother-in-law enjoyed doing was to collect fire-wood, so that was what she used to do.

After evening prayers and a short hymn, Jongile's mother turned to Nontombi. '*Nontombi, nceda ukhaphe uNowam aye kulungisa indawo yokulala ka Jongile.* Nontombi, please go with Nowam' – she was using my new name – 'to Jongile's rondavel to make their sleeping mattress.'

Before this moment, I had not thought that this might happen. Was I now to sleep with this man? I felt scared of what was going to happen. I was so embarrassed that I felt my mouth go dry and my ears start to ring. I did not speak a word as Nontombi walked me to my husband's rondavel.

I had not expected this, not at all. Not so soon.

When we got there, Nontombi opened the door to let me in and then, without saying anything, left. I walked inside, my throat still dry and tight. Jongile was sitting next to the fire.

He was in a very good mood. I looked around the room and saw that the bed was already ready. I did not have to make the mattress after all. The black pot over the wood fire was topped to the rim with hot water for bathing, and the room was filled with thick, choking smoke.

Jongile was smiling at me. 'Come, Nomfusi,' he said. 'I have already finished washing.' He pointed to the black pot. 'There is plenty of hot water for you to clean yourself in now.'

I looked at this man who was telling me to undress in front of him. I felt very shy, but not in a bad way. I realised then that, despite not wanting to marry him, I did have feelings for him. His dark skin and bright smile still made my skin tingle. But I was still young, and not ready for feelings of passion.

I had never before taken my clothes off in front of a man. It made me feel very uncomfortable, so I told him I would take the water outside and wash there.

'No, Nowam,' he said. 'You are not going to wash yourself out there in the cold. Don't be shy! You are my wife now.'

My mouth still felt very dry, but I did manage to speak. 'No. I am not your wife. Why do you keep on stealing me from my home?' My feelings for him were not strong enough to make me feel happy with being away from home. I told myself not to cry, but I felt that my tears were not far off.

'My mother will be worried for me again,' I said, my words getting stuck in my mouth. 'I have never been without her. And I never have been in one bed with a man.'

But Jongile shook his head. 'No, Nowam. She knows you are here with me. I took you this time because, while I am working to pay the lobola, I will not take the chance that another man will come for you instead.'

But I did not want to hear it. I dragged the basin outside with me, took off the long dress of my mother-in-law and bathed quickly by the light of the round, silver moon. It did not take long and I came back into the rondavel, shivering with cold.

Jongile laughed. I kept quiet.

He took me by the arm and pulled me down on the bed, covering me with thick blankets. He lifted the glass from the paraffin lamp and blew out the flame. He whispered softly to me as I was lying there, blinking in the dark.

Then he came very close to me. Never before had I been so close to a man. He said he would not be hard on me, that he loved me. That he wanted a child from me. I felt his rough breath on my face. I was so very scared of the moment he was going to touch my breasts.

I did not want this. I was frightened. Our parents always told us that we must never allow a man to touch us unless we were married. That our bodies belonged to our parents. I told him I did not want him to do this to me, but my words did not stop him. When I moved away from him, Jongile grabbed my thumb, twisting it.

'You are still a child, Nowam,' he whispered in my ear. 'And now you belong to me.'

My first time. It was horrible. For the first time in my life, I had come to hate my own body.

When it was over, I couldn't sleep. I was crying. I kept thinking that I was a virgin no longer. I was now a married woman. Then I thought, *Oh, Jesus. What if this man does not want me anymore? Like those other women he had before? What if he throws me away? What is to become of me then?*

I did finally fall asleep, waking up very early the next morning. The first morning with my husband. A new beginning of a new life. There would be many mornings when I would wake up like this. With a man beside me in my bed. *Oh, Mama. I wish I was with you. In your bed. Under your blankets.*

But I wasn't, and I would never be again. That part of my life was over. My home, my Mama, my life with the trees and the birds and the sheep in the fields and all those things that I had known and loved my whole life had, in one night, disappeared, as if I had woken up from a dream.

Then I felt the pain.

My body was sore all over. Every part of it. My thumb was swollen. It was the same finger I had once hurt in school while I was playing netball with the other children. When I got home, Mama had taken a sharp shaving blade and slit that finger to make it bleed. She said that that made the pain go away, and it had done that.

As a *makoti* I knew it was my job to get up and make coffee for everybody, so I silently dressed myself in that long dress and slipped out of the room while Jongile was still sleeping. It was a beautiful morning, the red of the sun streaming from the east, and for a moment I stood still, looking at it. The beauty. The peace.

After I knocked at the door of the main rondavel, I heard my mother-in-law call out to her lastborn son, who was a boy of nine years old, to let me in. He used to sleep with his father. 'Lunga! Lunga. Open the door for *makoti*!'

When the door opened I brought in the wood for the fire and greeted my parents-in-law. '*Molweni Tata, nawe Ma.*' I made the coffee and asked Lunga to take a cup to his father, as I was not allowed to give it to him myself. That was our culture. I was not allowed to even touch my father-in-law's hand.

I caught Ma staring at me as I moved around slowly, painfully. For the first time, I read emotion in her eyes. Understanding, compassion, sympathy. She told me to go back to Jongile's rondavel and not work that day. She was very kind to me.

At first I didn't want to go back to my bed because I thought it might be a trick to find out if I was lazy. But looking into her face again, I saw I was wrong, so I was glad to leave.

Jongile was still sleeping and for a long time I just sat there, watching him. My husband. When he finally woke up, he turned to me and smiled, telling me good morning and asking if I had slept well. '*Hayi, ubhontsi wam ubuhlungu,*' I replied. 'No, I did not. And my thumb is sore.'

He said he was sorry, that he had not meant to hurt me like that.

I told Jongile what Mama used to do, asking him to do the same. He took a very sharp blade and made a small cut in my sore thumb to make it bleed. A few minutes later, the pain slowly faded away.

But it did not take away the ache in the root of my soul.

Every day since then, from early morning to late evening, I cooked, cleaned, swept the house, fetched water from the spring, and collected wood with my mother-in-law, which we tied together with ropes into bundles. Then we put these bundles on our heads and carried them home.

I also did the washing for Ma, but I was not allowed to do it for her husband. It was also not allowed for me to touch my father-in-law's dish of food, or his mug of coffee. I had to ask one of the other girls or boys to do that. I could also not sweep his side of the house, which was to the left side of the door. All of that is part of our Xhosa culture. As a young *makoti,* those were the things to respect.

Every day, all those days, it made me so scared to see that the sun was about to go down, knowing what Jongile was going to do to me at night. Even though I knew that I did feel love for this man, my husband. I liked to be held by him, but I didn't want to do those other things.

So that is what my life became as a young *makoti.* So different to what I had imagined.

10
The most embarrassing moment in my life

About two weeks later, on a day when Jongile was in Queens-town, my brother, Mtshini, and my uncle's son, Siphelo, arrived unexpectedly at the home of my in-laws. Naturally, I was very happy to see my brother and cousin, even if I knew that his visit could bring trouble. When a family member shows up without warning, it usually means that there is a problem that needs to be talked about.

I quickly made them some tea and, while they waited, fetched my mother-in-law. My father-in-law had gone to his employer's stock camps early that morning after noticing vultures flying over them. Usually this meant that an animal had died, and that the birds were feeding on the carcass.

While my mother-in-law welcomed them into her home, Boniwe ran to the fields to tell her father he had visitors. I remember taking a deep breath when Mtshini asked for a second cup of tea. I didn't know my mother-in-law that well yet, and I was worried that she would think my brother was greedy.

When my father-in-law finally arrived, I was asked to leave while my family and in-laws discussed the problem. A little later, I was called back.

'Nowam,' said my mother-in-law. 'Please sit down and read this letter to my husband. I cannot see properly.' My father-in-law, like Mama, had never been to school and could not read. And as Ma's eyes gave her trouble, I had to read the letter for her.

Right away, I saw that the letter was written in Nomi's careful handwriting. A letter from home! Actually, it was a letter from Mama, but she had asked Nomi to write it for her.

I took the piece of paper and began to read. It was addressed to Mtshini.

Mrs Nose Kedama
Hukuwa General Dealer,
P O Whittlesea,
Via Queenstown

My dear son,

We are all very well here at home this evening. We have been sitting outside, where it was quiet and warm and where we could look up at the shiny stars in the wide heavens.

Mtshini, I write this letter to you to tell you that Nomfusi has been taken away by Amaqwambi's son, Jongile, to be his wife. She was carried off by him to his parents' house. Nomfusi came back home, and luckily Jongile had not touched her. She was still a virgin when she got back. I think those people know the tradition.

They then brought three cows and will bring three more, but they did not say when. So Nomfusi had to go back with him. The lobola is ten cows in total.

Nomfusi is worried about school, and she said that if she can get the chance, maybe she can now do correspondence classes.

Good luck, my son.
From your Mama,
Nose

After I finished reading the letter, Mtshini spoke.

'That is why I am here with my cousin. First of all, my sister is a schoolgirl. She was a virgin and I pray that for God's sake she still is. I wanted to help her to pay for her education, but now your son has carried her away from home to be his wife. Secondly, we hear that your son already had two other wives. And now the *lobola* has not even been paid in full!'

I looked at him nervously. My brother was getting very angry.

'Who do you people think you are, playing fools with other people's children? I do not want to hear another word spoken about it! I am taking my sister home with me, and I hope for your sake that your lover boy has not touched my sister!'

After these angry words, my cousin, Siphelo, spoke. 'Nomfusi, if you have any clothes or other things of your own here, go and pack them and come with us.'

I was so confused and embarrassed. I remember thinking to myself, what must I do now? I felt guilty and scared. Mtshini obviously did not know that Jongile had already lain with me, and that now I was, surprisingly, starting to feel love for this handsome man. He was always joking and cheerful and showed me great affection, treating me like I was a very fine crystal glass that could break just like that. He used to say that. And then he would say that if I, the crystal glass, was to fall and shatter, he too would fall to pieces and would stay a bachelor forever. Those were the words he used.

My husband had a very tender side to him. The only thing I did not like about him was what he did to me at night. That was so painful and disgusting. I wished that he would just talk to me and touch me softly, not that other thing.

I stood up and sighed. I had no idea what to say. Then I looked at my parents-in-law.

'Nomfusi, why are you sighing? Let's go!' Siphelo almost spat out those words.

'*Kahle! Kahle nyana!* Please, wait my son. Calm down!'

My father-in-law stood up and tried to speak to my brother, but Mtshini was so angry now that he said, 'You can tell your son to start looking for his type of woman! The type who is second-hand, like him!'

I was really getting very scared now, thinking to myself, *Oh, Lord, this must be the most embarrassing thing that will ever happen to me. How do I tell him that Jongile has already slept with me?*

'Come, Bhuti. You must go,' I said, taking Mtshini by the arm. I was afraid my brother would explode if he knew.

But my father-in-law interrupted. '*Mamela, nceda.* Listen, please. Leave our daughter-in-law here with us. Tomorrow, I shall go to my boss and ask to telephone my son in Queenstown.'

'Just tell your son that my sister is not his type,' Mtshini said over his shoulder as he marched out of the rondavel in anger.

I followed him out towards their bicycles and heard my cousin Siphelo whisper that the time was getting late and that it would be difficult to ride the long way home with me on the bike.

'What do you suggest we do then?' Mtshini asked, a little less sure of himself.

'Let's leave Nomfusi here, as the old man said, and then she can walk home during the day, starting in the morning. Is that all right, Nomfusi?'

I nodded, relieved.

'We want you back home,' Siphelo carried on. 'We believe that this man is not right for you.'

I told them that I did want to go home, to go back to Mama and to finish my education, but that Mama and my uncle had told me I must marry Jongile because the place of a girl is with her husband and to bear his children. I know that it had been difficult for Mama to tell me this, because she also wanted me to get a good education.

But I did not tell them about the other thing.

I felt relieved that my brother did not ask me if I was still a virgin. I don't even think the thought had crossed his mind that Jongile would have done that, so I watched them go on their bicycles. And I was torn between my feelings. *Where do I belong?* I thought. *And what must I do?*

11

Sneaking back home for the second time

Three days after my brother and cousin visited my in-laws, I sneaked back home for the second time. It was very early in the morning when I left. It was May, and very, very cold. Already, the cockerels outside were rejoicing about the coming day. It was the time of day we Xhosa people call *ukukhala kweenkuku zokuqala*. The first crowing of the roosters.

I had packed a few things the night before, without anybody noticing, and quietly left the rondavel, my small bag hidden under my dress. If anyone asked me where I was going, I would say I was going into the bushes to relieve myself.

With Jongile away in Queenstown, it was easy to steal away without anyone seeing. I crept along that gravel road quietly, hoping that no one would hear me. No one did. I was excited about going back home, but I wasn't looking forward to the long journey without a bike. I was hoping that a passing farmer might give me a lift, but no car came by. It was too early in the morning for anyone to go on that road.

The cold made my teeth click, but the stars shone brightly and kept me company. They made me feel a little better, and stayed with me until daybreak winked on the horizon. Just before that morning star went out in the sky, I sang her a song of thanks for watching over me.

'*Laphuma ikhwezi*
Laphum' ikhwezi lokusa
Ikhwezi
Ntombi yezulu khanyisa
Khanyisa ntombi yezulu.

There appears the morning star
There appears the morning star
The star, the star, daughter of the sky!
Light, light, daughter of the sky!
There comes the crack of dawn,
Beautiful morning star.'

In those days it was so nice to be able to walk home alone without being scared. Women and girls held no fear of being raped. No. In those days, if you saw a man on the road you'd be glad to have someone to walk with. Of course, that has all changed.

My brother was very happy to see me when I got home. He was laughing and hugging me. Mama, although very pleased that I was back, was keeping quiet. I glanced at her while Mtshini was talking. It was not easy to tell what she was thinking. *Can you see that I am no longer a child, Mama? Do you know that I am truly a woman now?*

'If Jongile does not bring any more cattle, you are not going back there again, Nomfusi,' Mtshini said. *Oh, Mtshini!* I thought. *You do not know what I do. That I have already been taken. That my husband did not wait.*

But I did not say anything.

Two days later, Jongile rode Kombuis to my home looking for me, and when he arrived my uncle and brother took him to the cattle kraal where they could speak to him in private. I was waiting inside the house, wondering what they were saying. After a short wait, Mtshini came out of the kraal where my uncle Jonga, my two aunts, Maradebe and Khethiles, and some of my cousins and other relatives were waiting.

'Nomfusi, Nomfusi! Come here, please!' I heard my aunt Maradebe say.

'Yes, aunt.'

I followed her to where some of the other women were sitting, and there was asked if Jongile had slept with me. The men were not there when she asked me.

I answered truthfully.

That is when my family came to a final agreement with my husband. I guess that when they knew that I was no longer a virgin, they also knew that I could never come home. Not without being disgraced. Any chance of Mama or my uncle changing their minds had been destroyed.

There was no going back.

So Jongile's offer of another three head of cattle was accepted and, as punishment for having slept with me without my family's permission, my husband had to pay them a money fine and the lobola was raised by one extra cow. One young cow for my virginity.

Before Jongile left the kraal, my uncle and brother told him that they were also keeping Kombuis there until he paid the fine to punish him for sleeping with me. They said that they would look after him until payment was made.

I actually felt a bit sorry for that horse, because I knew that Jongile and he were very close. Kombuis was stamping his legs on the ground, and he was neighing wildly. I think he knew that his owner was not taking him home, and he was not happy with that.

I felt strange inside as I watched Jongile walk home. I am not sure how to say it. All I had wanted until then was to be back at home with Mama and not stay with Jongile, but now, when he was going, I did not feel as happy as I thought I would.

I watched my husband go until he was only a little dot in the distance. Then I turned around to his horse. Kombuis was running around madly in circles inside the kraal, blind with fury that his owner had left him. It made me cry. I cried for the fear that the horse was feeling, and also a bit for myself. Something was not right. No, not right at all.

The very next day, Jongile rode his father's horse back to my home to pay the fine and to take Kombuis back with him. I don't remember how much he had to pay. He looked very dashing as he arrived on his father's horse that day. This horse was a blackish-red mare with a trimmed mane. She was not as fiery as Kombuis.

Horses were very valuable in those days, for when it was the time of the hard snow, the snow that would not melt away, cars could not go past on those gravel roads. Then these horses would take their owners to the distant shops for flour, tea, coffee and sugar. At Jongile's farm, other rations like mealies, tobacco, mealie meal and milk were brought in by van every month by my father-in-law's employer.

This day, when Jongile had come back to my home, he brought tobacco for my aunts as a sign of respect. In my culture it is custom to bring something like tobacco or food when you visit someone's house, and my aunts had asked him to bring them tobacco for their husbands and for a few of the older women who smoked. In those days, younger women never smoked cigarettes, although the older ones sometimes did.

After my husband had given them this tobacco and joked with them a bit, he walked to the kraal to fetch his horse. Kombuis became excited when he saw his owner. He was neighing and stamping his feet like the day before, but this time it was in a happy way. His ears were up high as he watched Jongile come into the kraal and he calmed down when my husband climbed on his back.

'Aren't you coming with me, Nomfusi?' Jongile asked. 'I really miss you, and I mean that! Why don't you come with me to my home, for you are the only woman I have truly wanted.'

What could I say? I told him that I would do as my family wanted me to do, and that they wanted me back with them for now.

'All right, then,' Jongile said. 'When my father brings the rest of the lobola, they will let you come to me. I love you, Nomfusi.' I felt shy and looked away. 'Please look after our unborn baby for me, Nomfusi.'

I got a shock when he said that. What is this man talking about? But before I could ask him what he meant, my husband clicked his tongue and, holding the reins of his father's horse in his right hand, he commanded Kombuis to go.

'Come, boy,' he said gently. 'Take me home.' And then he was gone.

Three days later, I noticed that two riders were coming our way. I was on my way back from the windmill to fetch water and had a very full bucket of water balancing on my head. I could make out three cows plus one horse without a saddle being herded towards me in a great cloud of fine dust.

Jongile's father and Tata July! My husband's father had brought with him his friend, the same man who had let me run back home on that stolen bike. They had come to pay lobola.

I stood there for a few moments, not moving as I saw them come closer and closer. I can still see it in front of me. As if it were happening now, like on television. Three cows and a horse. Some more cattle to pay the lobola. To pay the bride price. To pay for me.

Hearing the sounds of hooves and the mooing of the cattle, my aunts and cousins came from their homes and the fields, ululating and beating their shawls on the ground in celebration. '*Halala, halala, ukuzala kukuzolula. Zangena iinkomo zentombazana. Halala!* Here comes the cattle for the girl!'

I saw Mtshini's wife, Nune, and my cousin Bafana's wife, Maradebe, chanting and looking very happy. I just stood there, silently, that full bucket of water still balancing on my head. The air was thick with dust that settled on the bushes and trees of my home. Mama had come out of the hut, looking confused. And, for once, the birds stopped their beautiful song.

The second part of the lobola was here, and even though it hadn't yet been paid in full, I was officially allowed to go to my in-laws. To live at my in-laws' home as Jongile's wife. The remaining cattle were to be paid whenever my husband had a chance.

I had to go.

Part 2
My married life
1959 to 1966

'Then, when all the people have gone to bed and his
kinsmen have left, the man comes to you, while your
heart is still heavy with the words that have rained
down on you, because you know you have not
married only the man, you have married into his
family. From now on, you are under their roof.'

Elsa Joubert
The long journey of Poppie Nongena, 1980

1

Going to my marriage home

I left my home forever a week after that day. Even though I did go back to visit Mama from time to time, from that moment on I was a married lady with a new home, a new husband and new in-laws. I was Jongile's wife.

Mama had packed a suitcase for me and told Kholeka, my sister Ntemntem's daughter, to go with me. That was our custom. To escort the *makoti* to her new family. It had been agreed that Kholeka would stay with me at my in-laws for another week, after which Jongile would give her a lift home in his motorcar.

Kholeka was two years younger than me. She was a nice girl, and very much like my older sister, Ntemntem. I had always got on well with her and enjoyed laughing and joking with her. Kholeka could be shy one minute and gossipy the next, but she never lost her sense of humour.

Mama had also packed a bag for this niece of mine, and a basket of food. This was done because Kholeka was to stay as a guest with my parents-in-law for a whole week, and so, to respect them, she would be bringing them food and gifts.

We left on a Monday at around midday. The sun was high, sweeping its bright rays over me. It was a source of comfort to know that despite my leaving home and Mama we would still be together under the same sun.

Saying goodbye was the hardest part. Mama walked with us as far as the windmill, from where Kholeka and I carried on to the bus stop, which was still about an hour's walk away. As I stood there, with a suitcase on my head and the food basket in my hand, Mama hugged me tightly to her breast.

'*Uze uhloniphe abantu bomzi mntwana wam ukuze ube namathamsanqa.* Respect your in-laws, my child, so that you are blessed. My heart aches for you leaving me. Goodbye.'

The tears were coming now, even though I had been trying so very hard to swallow them back. I didn't want Mama to see that I was so unhappy to leave home. But even today, it is difficult for me to think about that moment without feeling very sad. Because now I know what lay ahead of me, what I was going towards when I got on that bus. Who knows what would have happened if I had not left home at that age? Where would my life have gone instead?

Today I am about the same age as Mama was that day when I left her, and as a grown woman I can better understand how she must have felt. Watching me, her daughter, her lastborn, go. I know, as a mother of grown children myself, how hard it is to let a child go. To see them walking down their own path. It is like a wound inside that never heals.

The bus arrived about half an hour after we got to the bus stop. It was the only transport for rural people to get to Queenstown and beyond. Well, other than walking or cycling, of course.

'*Niyaphina?*' the bus driver asked. 'Where are you going?'

'Nkaloemdaka,' I replied. This was between where the white-owned farms ended and the areas that were not so much developed started.

We got off the bus some time later, at three-thirty in the afternoon. I know that that was the time because I asked the bus driver. We still had a four-hour walk ahead of us. 'Come, we must walk quickly,' I said to Kholeka. 'I do not want to ask anybody for a place to sleep tonight, and if we hurry we will still get there before darkness falls.'

Kholeka looked alarmed when she heard the distance we still had to go. I don't think she had realised how far Jongile's home was. But there was nothing she could do. I put my suitcase on my head and carried the basket with baked bread, roasted chicken, sugar, coffee, tea and sweets under my arm.

As we walked, Kholeka soon cheered up and we talked and laughed and sang all the way there. It made the time go much faster and the walk far less long. We sang as we walked.

'Yhu! Yhu! Yhu! Solala phi?
Yhu! Yhu! Yhu! Solala phi?
Eli langa liya tshona solala phi.
Ah! Ah! Ah! Where do we sleep?
Ah! Ah! Ah! Where do we sleep?
The sun is setting, where do we sleep?'

It was the same song I had sung that day when Mama, Mama Cidi and I had gone to the thatch farm where I had met Jongile for the first time. It felt so long ago. When we finished singing, Kholeka stopped walking and turned to me. 'Nomfusi, tell me. Do you love this man you are marrying?'

It was not an easy question to answer. I thought about it for a while, then told her that I *did* love him, but that I was also scared of him.

'Why?' she asked.

'I think it is because I feel shy with him,' I finally said.

'But why?'

I didn't know how to answer any more. We walked in silence for a bit, and then I said, 'I think I am shy because I don't know if Jongile really loves me. This marriage means I have to leave all the things I care for. My home. Mama. My schooling.' As I spoke, it felt as though I was making sense of what I felt by saying the words. 'And all for this man who has been married twice before. I do love him now, I think. He is nice, and always joking. But these things all scare me.'

I think she understood.

We arrived at my parents-in-law's home at about eight o'clock. It was already dark, but the moon was out and its light showed us the path like a light from heaven. The same moon-light that shone on Mama at home.

When we were still a little distance away from the rondavel, I heard their dog begin barking. It was not an angry sort of bark, but a happy one. I do not remember the name of that dog, but it was a sheepdog. Black and white and very friendly. By that time, he and I were already friends. He must have smelled it was me.

My parents-in-law were just about to start evening prayers when they heard the barking of the dog. My father-in-law came outside to see who was there.

'*Awu! Nguwe molokazana!* I knew that there must be someone familiar,' he said. 'That kind of barking always tells me when a friend arrives at my home. Please come in, my children. You must be very tired!'

Both my parents-in-law, as well as Boniwe and Nontombi, were very happy to see us. Jongile was not home that evening, as it was a Monday. He had left for Queens-town the night before.

'Who is this young woman?' my mother-in-law asked when we came inside the rondavel.

I told her that she was my sister's daughter, and that her name was Kholeka.

'Ah!' she said. 'I can see that she is your relative! She has the same light skin as you, Nowam. You must have San blood running inside your veins.'

She then turned to my niece. 'Hello, Kholeka! How are you?'

By now Kholeka was very tired after our long journey. 'I have never walked such a distance before, Ma,' she yawned. 'And I do not think I will ever want to do that again!'

We all laughed. 'That cannot be true,' I said to her. 'How long does it take to walk from your home to mine?'

97

She had to admit that it would take her from sunrise to sunset, and then she too started laughing. That evening we shared a supper of samp and vegetables, and some of the roasted chicken and bread that Mama had packed into the basket.

'I will send Jongile a message that you are here, Nowam,' my mother-in-law said. 'I am sure that he will be very happy with the news.'

When my husband returned from work that Saturday morning, he was indeed very pleased to see me. 'Now that you are here,' he said with a big smile on his face, 'we can start our new life as husband and wife together. It will be a good marriage, Nowam!'

All I could do was pray that he was right.

2

The first time I found out I was pregnant

Late one afternoon in July 1959, less than three months after I came to Jongile's home as his *makoti*, I found out that I was pregnant. I had just brought some wood to the main rondavel to make a fire when my mother-in-law asked me if I was feeling all right.

'*Ewe, Ma*,' I replied. '*Ndiphila kakuhle.* I am well. Why?'

She looked closely at me. 'Because you don't look so well. Are you getting enough sleep?'

I hadn't even thought that I might be pregnant. Not at all. Even though I had been feeling a little tired and nauseous, I had told myself that it was probably nothing. But it was not nothing. I was carrying Jongile's child.

When I told my husband's mother that I had been feeling sick in the mornings, she clapped her hands and began to laugh.

'*Molokazana umithi!*' she exclaimed happily. 'Daughter-in-law, you are pregnant! I am very happy!'

But I was not happy about this, not at all. A child! What was going to happen when I had another person, a baby, relying on me? Then the wonder of it began to sink in. I remember feeling quite excited. *I hope it will be a girl*, I thought.

When Jongile heard the news on the weekend, he was dancing with joy. 'My one and only wife! I knew! I knew!' he laughed. 'I am so happy that you are giving me a child! And I don't mind if it is a boy or a girl. It does not matter to me. Imagine! Our first baby!'

And I was happy for him. I could see that it meant the world to my husband to have a child with me.

One Saturday a few weeks later, Jongile told me that he was throwing a party the following weekend. He asked me to brew the beer. I felt a little foolish, because I had never made *umqombothi* before, and I had no idea how to make it.

When I told him, my mother-in-law said, '*Hayi, mntwana wam. Sukuhlupheka. Ndiza kufundisa.* No, my child. Don't worry. I will teach you.'

That Monday, Jongile's mother told me to grind dry mealies in between two stones. When that was done, I took twenty gallons of warm water and soaked those mealies overnight, mixed with *imithombo,* malt.

The following morning, we cooked that mixture and let it cool before adding more malt to make it brew. Finally, I ran it through a bag that was made of grass and left it for three days. After this, the African beer was ready to be drunk.

By the morning of the party, we had killed and cooked a chicken and had prepared all sorts of things to eat like bread and sweets and roast *koek.* This food was put on a wooden table against the wall. Later on, when the party had started, we would sell the food to the guests at a price that they offered. It was customary to do this to help the hosts pay for the party.

I was excited. It was the first time I was to meet Jongile's friends and the rest of his relatives. It was also the first time that they would see me. I think his friends knew that my husband had loved me for a long time before I went to his home, because lots of boys and girls came up to us, saying that we looked a very happy husband and wife. I felt quite special then. It was the first time I was introduced to other people as my husband's wife. It was also a bit funny. I still thought of myself as a child, but now I had a husband, and I was a married lady.

Then the music started. At these parties there was always lots of different music. Several of the boys had guitars and played lovely songs that everyone would sing and clap to. Jongile, too, was very musical. He played many instruments.

Then the time came for buying the food and other items on the table. One of the boys said that he wanted to buy the chicken that had been killed earlier in the day and was now lying roasted on a plate. He offered two shillings for it. Another boy raised the bid to three, and so it went. I can't remember how much that chicken went for in the end.

When all the sweets and roast *koek* and other food had been sold, Jongile raised his hand. As everybody quietened down, he said loudly, 'One shilling for one kiss. I will pay one shilling … for Phakama to kiss me on the lips!'

Everybody was laughing, looking at Phakama to see if she would do it. Other boys also started bidding, but in the end it was my husband who won the bet. He got up, strolled over to that girl and kissed her while everyone looked.

Another ripple of laughter went through the party. The only one who was not laughing was me. Some of those boys and girls turned to look at me while my husband was kissing that girl, trying to see how I felt. Well, I didn't like it. I didn't like it at all. But I did not take it badly, either. After all, I told myself, it was only a joke. A way to raise some money for the food and drink at the party. I did not think it was serious.

But still, I did not laugh.

Phakama was not a nice-looking girl. She had a short and fat body, but the boys liked her all the same. When my husband had finished his kiss, he came to sit with me and put his arm around my shoulders. I was, by now, frowning, but he laughed off the kiss as a joke. I didn't know then what I know now. That Jongile and Phakama were going to be involved together.

That evening, after the party, we talked about Phakama.

'That girl! She has the body of an ant!' my husband laughed, drawing me closer to him.

I asked him what he meant by that and, watching him outline the overgrown bulges of an ant's body, I began to smile. Then I realised that he was talking about her big backside! So we laughed my worries away together.

But only a few years later, Phakama bore my husband a baby of her own. How could he? Was it because he was lonely all those weekdays in Queenstown while I was living at his home? I never knew.

That summer was very hot. Fields that were once green suffered silently as the sun burnt the grasses until they were a dull, yellow colour. The soil was loose under our feet, and even the chickens, as they scrambled around for food, kicked up dust from under their raking claws.

Everything was very dry. By the time the summer rains came, I was about six-and-a-half months pregnant. The weight of the child growing inside me left me weary most of the time and I, like everyone else, was looking forward to rain. The clouds were looking as pregnant and bloated as I was. It was time for their burden to be relieved, and for all life beneath to be nourished.

One Sunday, our preacher at the Methodist church, who was also the schoolteacher at the local primary school, told us that we were all to climb the Nkonkobe Mountains the following week to pray for rain. The next week, on the day of the climb, worshippers came from all over, laughing and cheering and chatting, carrying bibles and buckets of *umqombothi*. There were many people at the gathering. I recognised some of them from the farm where my in-laws worked.

We first went to church to say a short prayer and to sing a hymn. Then we started the slow climb up the mountain. When we finally got there, the preacher said, '*Masiphakame.* Let us stand up and be quiet! We all know why we are here today, for our land is thirsty and needs rain!'

I was standing next to a very fat lady, who looked like she was feeling very tired after that steep climb. 'That man,' she said, wiping her forehead, 'can't he wait a few seconds so that we can rest a little first? I am feeling quite breathless, and you, *makoti*,' she pointed at my bulging tummy, 'you must be tired, too!'

She then pointed at a rock and said that we should sit there together, but before I could do so, my mother-in-law stopped me.

'Don't sit on that rock, Nowam!' she said. 'It will not be healthy for you or the baby to sit on that rock.' I wasn't sure why she thought that, but I obeyed and, holding my tummy with both my hands, I joined her in listening to the preacher.

'We are here to ask our Lord for rain,' he said. 'So my brothers and sisters, let us all get down on our knees and pray. There is nothing more powerful than to offer our prayers to the Lord. Let us pray!'

I tell you, it was difficult for me to get on my knees like that without falling over! But with Ma's help, I managed. After the prayer, the preacher thanked everyone for coming and then it was time to drink the beer. I only had a little *umqombothi*. I did not usually drink this, only on a special occasion or at a traditional feast, but on this day Ma handed me a small cup and I drank with all the other people there.

When everyone had finished drinking the water and *umqombothi*, we made our way down the mountain to go back home. Then a miracle happened. The dark clouds burst open, drumming on the parched earth. It was pouring with rain! Everyone began cheering and laughing and singing.

'Jesus never disappoints his people!'

'Thank you, Lord! Blessed art thou, Lord!'

'Praise be to the Father!'

That was the first time I prayed for rain. It was the first time I had been part of a ceremony like that, and I have to say, I was impressed. Over the next few days, the rain brought back the green to the land and the grass in the fields. It was a humbling time.

One day soon after, my husband told me he wanted to give up his job in Queenstown and look for work at one of the farms nearby. Then he and I could live together.

'I never see you, Nowam,' he said to me. 'You are always working hard at my home with my parents, but I want you with me.'

When my husband went to speak to his parents, they were not happy to hear his plans.

'*Hayi!* No!' said his mother. 'Who is going to work here then, for us? Nowam is our *molokazana*, our daughter-in-law. We have helped you with our cattle to pay the lobola for her so that she could help us here, and now you want to take her away!'

My mother-in-law was about fifty years old at that time, and I think she was scared that she would not be able to cope with the work if I left. Her husband was two years older. But finally they did agree, and Jongile took me with him to a farm where he hoped to find work.

We left early in the morning on a beautiful day. The sun was out and the sky was a clear blue and there wasn't a whisper of wind. After many hours of walking on the greenest of grass, we found ourselves at the foot of the mountain called Nkonkobe. This mountain was so high that it was full of snow in winter. But not this day, of course, as it was summer and the weather was warm.

'Come, Nowam,' my husband said to me. 'Let us and our baby rest here, in the shade of this lovely tree.'

We rested a while before making love under that tree. I hadn't really wanted to, but Jongile said that it would make the baby feel strong. In some traditions, the man leaves the woman alone when she is carrying his child, but in ours the husband takes his wife until she is very close to giving birth.

Afterwards, I asked my husband if I could remove my *doek*, as my head was itching badly. '*Bhuti kaNontombi*,' I said, 'please can I take it off?'

In those days, while I was working so hard doing the house

cleaning, collecting wood, fetching water and cooking for seven people, the tight *doek* wrapped around my head troubled me at times. I had it on day and night, and I had little time to wash or comb my hair so, like many *makotis*, I suffered badly from head lice.

Jongile told me to put my head on his lap, took off the *doek* and began to comb gently through my short curly hair with his slender fingers, picking the lice from my head as best as he could.

This is the kind of thing that made me love my husband so much. He was so gentle and kind, and he would give me so much attention. He listened to what I was saying and what was important to me. I don't know how many times I told him about how much I loved to watch the birds, and hear them singing, and he never tired of me saying those things.

Some time later, we set out again for this farm, getting there in the middle of the day. I was so relieved that we were there! It was a long way from the home of my parents-in-law, and we had walked all that time straight through the grass and the bushes. There was no proper path or road through this way, and it was so steep at places that I had to hold on to the shrubs, sometimes even sliding down on my bum, which was not that easy with my big tummy.

But then we were there. Jongile went straight to the house of one of the black workers that he knew, and then went off to speak to the white farmer to ask for a job. He was quite sure that there would be a job for him as he was a good mechanic. He knew how to take apart a car engine and fix it so that it was running again.

Well, he did get a job there, but we only stayed at that place for about two months. The pay was not good, so we left. I went back to his parents, and Jongile returned to his old job in Queenstown.

About two weeks after we came back, I started to feel sharp pain in my tummy. It was time. My baby was coming.

3

Giving birth to my first child

The pains began around midnight. As I lay there, waking up to what was happening, I heard the roosters crowing outside under the dark night sky. I listened to them for a few moments before turning over to wake Nontombi, who got up and went to fetch my mother-in-law.

I wasn't sleeping in my own room. During the week, when Jongile was in Queenstown, I slept in the main rondavel with my in-laws. At night, I used to wait until my father-in-law turned off the lamps before I could undress and go to sleep. This I was told to do by my mother-in-law out of respect for him. But as the day of giving birth drew closer, I moved into the room where Nontombi and Boniwe slept, as that was the place I was to have my baby.

Never before had I felt such pain! It felt as though someone was stabbing my tummy with a blunt dagger.

Ma came into the hut. 'Come, Nowam,' she said soothingly. 'Let me help you. Your child is near now.'

She quickly made a fire while helping me onto my knees. I wondered why Ma was making a fire when it was the middle of summer and the night air was still warm, but then she explained. 'Nowam, if you are hot and sweaty the baby will come quickly, and you will have a fast delivery.'

She moved my mattress so close to that fire that I almost

fainted from the heat. That is one of the things I remember best about that night, that sweltering heat. Strangely enough, I did not feel nervous, not at all. I trusted in my husband's mother because, like Mama, she had been a midwife for a long time and had brought many babies into this world.

The pains came and went as I knelt down over that mattress, coming and going, like crashing thunder. Ma said this meant that the baby must be a girl.

'It is always like that,' she said. 'When the pain goes on and off. Girls are lazy. They take a long time to come. Not like boys.'

Despite my pain, I smiled. 'Are you sure, Ma? Are you certain that this is a girl?'

That made me very happy. When I was still a child, and some of us schoolgirls spoke about having our own children, I would always tell the other girls that if I got married, I would want first a girl and then a boy. So if my mother-in-law was right about this, my wish to start with a girl had come true.

Hours passed. The stabbing pains came faster, closer to each other. My head was filling with mist. When I close my eyes, I can still see that room with me bending over that mattress, staring at the mud walls and trying to breathe over the smell of the smoke and heat of the fire.

And the pains!

Ma was there all the time, comforting me and telling me to push for my baby. I was writhing with the pain. She gave me some hot tea that she had made, but I didn't feel like drinking it. But she made me sip it slowly, telling me that it was a remedy made from special herbs to make the birth flow easily.

And then the pain started again. It was coming faster now. Faster and faster and faster.

'Here, my daughter-in-law,' she said. 'Take this empty bottle, and blow! Blow inside it with all the strength you have.'

Finally, with one last push, I gave birth to my first child.

The first person to touch this new life was my husband's mother. She took the baby and slapped her softly on the bottom, nodding and smiling at the wail that followed. Then I heard Ma laugh. It was a girl, she said.

A daughter!

I looked at my husband's mother. She was crying. I felt a little shy seeing her like this, so I looked away. When she stopped, she bathed the baby, helping me to wash too, and told me to properly clean and rinse my nipples. When this was done, she gave my baby to me, and showed me how to hold and breastfeed her.

It was a wonderful new experience to have my daughter drink from me. I was amazed that my body could give birth to a living human being, and then also give that little person the food it needed to grow strong and healthy. *I am a mother now! A mother to my firstborn child.*

It's very hard for me to describe my feelings during those first moments after my daughter's birth. I felt wonder. Amazement. And love. Yes. A world of love. Looking into the face of that child was like looking at a familiar stranger, someone I had known for a long time but had never seen before. Her little brown body so warm and trusting. So close to me. Her innocent eyes that also knew such truth. They reflected back to me warmth and understanding as if she, too, was feeling these same things.

It was the most beautiful moment of my life.

This great, complete happiness stayed with me for a very long time. Even today, when I think back to that moment, the tears rise from behind my eyes. Tears of happiness.

For the rest of that day, my mother-in-law looked after me very well. She made me some sorghum porridge to eat and sat with me, making sure that my baby and I were all right. Then she went to the river to pick a special plant that had fine, soft green leaves and reddish roots. I don't know what the name of that plant was, but after she boiled the roots, she got from it a juice that we called *isicakathi*. Ma gave a teaspoon of this juice to the baby, saying that it would help her tummy to go freely.

After this was done, Ma went towards a small cliff close to the cattle kraal to collect dry cow's dung and old, dried-up mouse droppings. Those wild mice had a lot of holes close to the kraal, and their droppings could easily be found lying outside of those holes, hardening in the sun. She collected all these and ground them over a flat stone. Then she mixed this powder with my breast milk to make a dough, which she then smeared on the baby's navel. That was the way of letting the navel fall off after a week or so.

Once it did fall off, it was Xhosa custom to bury it inside the main rondavel. If this doesn't happen immediately, or if the navel gets lost, bad luck will certainly come upon the child. But if the navel is buried inside the house, it is believed that this will prevent the child from not wanting to come back to his or her old home in the future.

I stayed in bed for a week to regain my strength after the birth. I was not allowed to leave at all, except to relieve myself in the bushes, and even then blankets and shawls covered my body and head, because as a new mother I was not to be seen by any men during this period. Apart from my husband, of course. But Jongile had just gone back to his job in Queens-town, and would only come home the next weekend.

After that week finally passed, I was very happy to get out of that room. By that time I was singing and laughing, putting on fresh new clothes to greet the world again. My mother-in-law showed me how to fasten the baby on my back using a long shawl that was tightly wrapped.

After that, for the first time since the birth, we went to see my father-in-law in the main rondavel. He had not seen his baby granddaughter yet, because that was our custom too. Only after that period of rest may the grandfather meet his grandchild.

It was a very happy moment. I don't think that I had ever seen my father-in-law show such joy as when he started singing and talking to this child. Both my in-laws were very fond of my baby. They were both laughing and laughing. My mother-in-law then began singing a very sweet lullaby for the baby, and I was touched by the emotion in her voice.

I had named my baby girl Thokoza, but, in Xhosa tradition, the first grandchild is named by the parents of the baby's father. So I could not call her the name I had chosen, and it was never used. The firstborn child belongs to the parents of the husband, and so it was my mother-in-law who named my baby a beautiful name. Lindiwe.

The reason for this first child belonging to the parents of the husband is that it was thought that the child would be taking care of them when they reached old age and were no longer able to take care of themselves.

Having that baby girl gave new meaning to my life. Purpose trickled all the way down into my body and soul. It was as if Lindiwe had always been with me. I could not imagine how I had lived without her for all that time that went before she came.

But soon I was reminded of how frail life is, and how quickly everything can change. One morning, not long after the birth, my in-laws went to church, while I stayed behind with Lindiwe. She was still so very small that I didn't want to take her anywhere yet.

My sweet baby had just woken up from her morning nap and, after she suckled a bit, I carried her to a basin that I had filled up with warm water for her bath. It was the first time I had ever bathed the baby by myself.

She enjoyed being in the water so much, and made all sorts of happy baby sounds as I cupped handfuls of water over her round, chocolate-coloured tummy. I loved bathing her.

Then some of the bathwater spilt into her little nostrils by accident. Her head, which was already covered by a thick crop of curly black hair, jerked back. She began to wail bitterly. I panicked. I knew that if the water had gone down into her lungs it could be very, very dangerous. *Oh, my God! Forgive me! My baby! Please, please, let her be all right!* I prayed.

I was shaking her, probably a bit too hard in my fear, blowing into those small nostrils. I didn't know what I could do. Luckily, it was only a very small amount of water. After a few seconds she stopped crying. She was all right! I felt bad about it, but I had also learnt to be so very, very careful.

When Jongile came home from Queenstown and saw his child, he was a very happy man. Like his father, I don't think I ever saw my husband smiling and laughing so much. Our baby clearly meant the world to my husband. He doted on her, as in later years he doted on all of his children. Whatever our problems, Jongile was a good father who loved his children as much as any father could.

He had brought all sorts of things from town for her. Nappies, baby soap and lots of other baby things. And for me there were pretty new nightdresses. I loved them.

So Jongile's family embraced their new granddaughter and my firstborn child with hearts full of love. And although I was happy about that, I couldn't help but feel a little bit sad that neither my Mama, or any of my other sisters or brothers, were there. This was their moment, too.

That Sunday morning, my mother-in-law said to Jongile and me, 'My son and daughter-in-law. This child is ours now, so you must now try and have another one for yourselves!' We all laughed.

It was one of the happiest times that I had there, at my in-laws. A time when we were all united by the birth of a beautiful, healthy baby girl. A moment where the future seemed full with all that was good and hopeful.

If only that had been so.

4

My marriage to Jongile

About three months after the birth of Lindiwe, my husband surprised me very much by asking me a question. Would I marry him?

Jongile and I were, of course, already married according to traditional custom, but our vows had not yet been exchanged in a church. 'We will visit your mother,' Jongile said happily on an unusually warm autumn morning. 'I want to tell her that I wish to marry her daughter, because I shall never be married again to another woman. You, Nowam, are the wife God has given me.'

'But why, *bhuti kaNontombi*?' I asked. 'Why do you want to marry me when we are already husband and wife, and I have borne you a child?'

But secretly I was very pleased that he asked me, and so of course I said yes. *Maybe this time he really means what he says. That I am the one and only true woman for him. Maybe those other two wives did not mean anything to him after all.* My husband's proposal meant a lot to me. It made me feel sure that I would not be thrown away, as he had thrown away those other two women. So, when we went to my Mama's home in his motorcar the next Saturday, I was very happy.

I will never forget that day.

Mama was outside, sweeping away the dirt outside the

rondavel in her long frock and black *doek*. When she heard Jongile's car, she raised her eyes and, for a moment, looked confused. Then, when she saw that it was me, Ntondo, her last-born child, her frown turned into a look of utmost joy. She dropped that broom, creating a small cloud of dust, and rushed towards the car to greet me. 'Nomfusi!'

And then she saw the baby. '*Yhu, yhu, yhu! Umzukulwana wam ndaza ndambona ekugqbeleni, mzise apha ndimbone!* At last, I get to see my grandchild. Bring her to me, I have been so longing to see her!'

Apart from Mziwakhe, Mama was alone at the house. Mama quickly called her firstborn grandson and, holding Lindiwe close to her breast, showed him his baby cousin.

While Mama and Mziwakhe were laughing and chatting with my husband, I quickly made a fire outside for tea. By this time, some of my other relatives, having heard the noise, had come rushing out of their homes to welcome us and congratulate us on our beautiful baby.

Mziwakhe left us to find a chicken to slaughter for supper. He did this because Mama's son-in-law was visiting her home, and he was to be respected. A special meal needed to be cooked that evening.

Once the chicken was killed, Mziwakhe plucked the feathers off its limp body and cut the pink meat into pieces. He then gave that chicken to me to cook in Mama's big black pot with potatoes, beans and pumpkin. These vegetables my husband had brought to Mama as a gift.

After we all had supper and the dishes had been cleaned outside, we sat in the rondavel to exchange our news. Lindiwe was already fast asleep in Mama's sleeping place. Mama had bathed her before we had had our meal, cradling my precious child until she had fallen asleep. Mama was so in love with this baby! She couldn't keep her eyes off her, and kept saying that Lindiwe was such a good little baby, and how much she looked like me and how well she was suckling.

'Ma,' Jongile said, 'I have come here today to speak with you about something very important.' He paused for a moment, stealing a quick glance in my direction. 'I have come to ask you for permission to marry your daughter. She is very special to me, and I would like us to be married in the church.'

Mama looked very surprised. It must have been one of the few times in her life that she was speechless. But then she smiled and told my husband that she would speak to my uncle. Then she asked him why he wanted to marry me in a church.

'Well, Ma, I have already married your daughter traditionally but now, because she is my one and only wife, I want to marry her before God.'

This made Mama very happy. She was fond of Jongile, even during those early days when I didn't want to be married to him. When I was still a schoolgirl. Back then, the only reason she had doubts about my marrying him was because I would be the third wife. And because she knew I wanted to finish my education. She always told me that I would be a very good schoolteacher.

My husband also liked Mama very much. I remember when he heard the news of her death in August 1989 he looked like a broken man. He said he felt terrible that he couldn't make it to her funeral. Because by that time, Jongile was a very sick man himself.

Two years after my mother passed away, my husband died. That was in 1991. Even though we were separated by then, we still spoke to each other. We did have children together, after all, and there were always things that needed to be spoken about.

But all of that was more than thirty years later. Thirty years since Jongile asked Mama for my hand in marriage. Where has the time gone?

That evening, I went with Jongile to the hut where a sleeping place had been made for him, telling him that I wanted to spend the night with Mama, like I used to. He agreed. 'All right, Nowam. Good night,' he said. 'I will see you tomorrow morning.'

Mama was so excited to have me and the baby sleep with her! It felt like a long time since I had been there, underneath her blankets, like I used to. It was like old times again, but even more special now that there were three of us under the same blanket.

We were chatting and laughing so much that we forgot about being silent for the baby. Lindiwe woke up and started crying.

'Hush, little baby,' Mama cooed. When Lindiwe didn't stop after a few minutes, she took her *hadi* and began to sing a very sweet song to her.

This *hadi* was a musical instrument that she had made herself. I don't know what the word for it is in English, but Mama had made it from a long stick with a calabash at the bottom. The stick was bent to make it curve, and it had one wire string that ran from one end of it across to the bottom of the calabash.

She had always liked playing on this instrument, even when we were small children, making it come alive by striking a thin stick across that string ever so softly. Now, as the first sweet notes danced in the air, Mama began singing a soft, sweet lullaby for my baby. It was a sad tune, about being lonely. When I was a child and she sang that song to me, I used to cry. It went

'*Thula bhabha, thula sana*
Thul'umam'uzoboya ekuseni
Thula bhabha thula sana
Uzodlul' entaben' emathafeni
Khukw'inkanyezi ekhokhel' utata
Emkhanyisela iindlel' eziy' ekhaya.

'Hush baby, hush baby
Hush, mother will come back in the morning
Hush baby, hush baby
She will cross the mountains and plains
There is a star that leads the father
Lighting his path coming home.'

After Mama died, Nomi took the *hadi,* and even today, when I go and visit my brothers and sisters in Queenstown, we sing this song together and cry because it reminds us so much of those sweet days.

Lindiwe stared at Mama with big brown eyes as she listened, her sweet face soft and silent, until finally sleep came over her like a soft blanket and her eyelids closed.

A little later Mama and I, too, went to sleep.

And so my husband and I had a church marriage in March 1960, nearly a year after he took me as his *makoti* and shortly after I had turned seventeen. The reverend of the Methodist church in Kamastone, a very pretty rural area not far from Whittlesea, performed the small ceremony and laughed and shook our hands after he pronounced us man and wife.

My mother-in-law made my wedding dress, which was a soft pale pink colour, especially for this day. With it I wore a wide-brimmed white hat and white shoes.

Jongile, too, looked very handsome. He was wearing a pair of black and grey checked pants with a pink shirt, white tie and a grey hat. When I looked at him during the ceremony and saw him looking so proud, a feeling of intense love passed through me.

The only sad thing was that Mama could not be there that day. She had not been feeling well and so had sent Nune, my brother's wife, instead. Ma was there, but not her husband, as he could not get away from his work at the farm.

And so, by the end of that day, I was officially married to Jongile. The man who changed the shape of my destiny.

5
The day I lost trust in my husband

I gave birth to my second baby a year later. Another girl, and again Ma helped me to deliver her. I was so very, very happy that this child was another girl. It was what I thought might happen, and was just as I had wished.

Thokozile was a beautiful baby, with a light complexion. She got that from my father-in-law. Mama, like me, had very fair skin, but my husband's father was even lighter. He was almost white, and very different from his wife, because Ma was very, very dark.

Much later on, Thokozile's skin turned much darker, to a more brownish coffee-bean colour. And she looked so much like her father! Exactly so. Even today, I cannot help but think of my husband when I look at her lovely face.

A few weeks after the birth of Thokozile, I began to visit Jongile in Queenstown. Up to that time, my husband came back home from his job every Saturday morning, while I was at my in-laws, nursing the baby.

Each time I went to visit him in Queenstown, Jongile first had to ask his parents' permission for me to go there to see him. They agreed, on condition that my visit was not too long. They depended on me a lot to do the cooking and cleaning, to look for firewood and fetch water and so on. I would make an effort to work very hard before going to Queenstown, and make sure that there was enough fresh water and firewood to keep them going long enough during the time I was away.

One Saturday morning, about six months after the birth of my second baby, Jongile came home from Queenstown with one of his friends and a girl whose father was a distant relative of mine. We were both from the Majola clan and were around the same age. This girl and I had gone to different schools, but we knew each other from concerts and sports gatherings and things. Her name was Yoliswa.

The strange thing was that, instead of coming and chatting to me, this relative of mine was avoiding me all of Saturday. She wouldn't even look at me as we were making supper! No, she just followed Nontombi around. I couldn't understand why she was acting like that, but I do remember thinking that perhaps she was just very shy.

The following day, Sunday, Nontombi and Yoliswa went to the river to fetch water for cooking. I had stayed behind to stamp the mealies. Outside, I heard my husband speaking to his mother. I was not really listening to what they were saying, but I stopped stamping those mealies when I heard my husband ask his mother a very strange thing, to take one of the beds back with him to his place in Queenstown. *Why would he want to do that?* I asked myself.

In those days, *makotis* didn't question their husbands or ask them why they did things. So I just kept quiet and watched Jongile that evening as he got ready to go back to Queenstown. After he had packed his clothes, he tied one of the beds onto the top of his car. When he saw me looking at him, he told me that he was taking the bed to his room in Queenstown for his cousin, who was staying with him while he looked for work in town.

I felt confused and unhappy. What was going on? I couldn't explain it, but something was not right, not right at all. I knew that this was not the truth. That evening, after my husband, his cousin and Yoliswa had gone, I was outside cooking supper over the fire when Nontombi came and sat by my side.

'Sisi,' she said in hushed tones. 'Please don't tell my brother what I am about to tell you, but I think there is something you should know.'

She looked behind her shoulder to make sure that no one was listening. As I waited for her to speak, I knew that it was something bad. My throat was feeling dry. I think that I already knew what she was going to say. That my husband was cheating on me with another woman.

'That girl who was here today, your relative, she told me that my brother is her boyfriend. She said that I mustn't tell anybody that she loves him!'

It felt as though my body had fallen into ice-cold water, clouding my mind and making my skin numb. On the one hand I could not believe it, but all my insides were telling me that it was true.

Why? *Why*? He said that I was his one and only true wife!

But I did not say that. I don't even remember what I said to Nontombi, if I said anything at all. She knew this news would upset me, but she also knew that I would want to know. And I did. I was grateful for her honesty and loyalty, and I told her so.

In those days, we would never even think of confronting our husbands with this sort of thing. Not like today, when young women are so much stronger. But I did want to find out for myself if all this was true, so the next morning I went inside the house to ask my mother-in-law for permission to visit my husband in Queenstown.

'But why, *molokazana*? Your husband just left this morning. Is anything wrong?'

I didn't know how to tell her, and I felt very ashamed about it, but I also knew that I could not tell her a lie. So I took a deep breath to tell her, but then Nontombi, who had come with me, spoke up first.

Ma was so shocked! She immediately said that I should go to my husband to try and find out what was going on.

'You must take Nontombi with you, Nowam,' my mother-in-law advised. 'If you leave tomorrow, in the afternoon, you will be at my sister's home by sunset. You can sleep there. She lives close to the bus stop, so you can catch the bus the next morning.'

So we packed a few things and left the next day at about noon. It was going to be a very long walk to my mother-in-law's sister, but from Ma's sister's house, it would take only a few minutes to walk to that bus stop.

That Tuesday was a chilly day. The sky was filled with fast-moving, angry clouds. A dark day for a dark secret to come to light. We walked quickly, even with me carrying Thokozile on my back. I had left Lindiwe with Ma. We struggled over those steep gravel roads that go up and down through the rural area near the Nkonkobe Mountains, and after about an hour I grew very tired. The baby was beginning to slide down my back and it became difficult for me to walk properly.

When Nontombi saw that I was battling with Thokozile, she stopped. 'Sisi,' she said. 'Let me carry the baby for a while. She is right down your back.'

I felt so sorry for poor little Thokozile when I saw how her soft right cheek was chafed. It had rubbed against my back during the walk, and she hadn't even cried. Nontombi took the baby and strapped her onto her back with a long shawl. We continued on our way.

We got to the home of my mother-in-law's sister just before dusk, feeling tired and thirsty. I had not met my husband's aunt before. Nontombi introduced us and said that we were on our way to see Jongile. She did not say why.

Ma Nomandla was a kind lady, with dark skin like her sister, but that is where their family resemblance stopped. While Ma was tall and slender, this lady was short and plump. She took us inside her rondavel and introduced us to her husband and two daughters. I don't remember their names or how old those girls were, but I think they were just slightly younger than Nontombi.

As it was already quite late, we sat down to supper. I was quiet, thinking about what might be waiting for me in Queenstown. Nontombi chatted about the news from home while we ate the stamped mealies and sugar beans. After this, my mother-in-law's sister laid down a mattress for us inside the house, which Nontombi, the baby and I shared. Thokozile was a good traveller. She had been happy throughout our walk and fell asleep easily without waking during the night.

I was up before Nontombi and Thokozile the following morning and, having been told the evening before where the wood was, I made a fire. I then took a black pot and filled it with water, putting it on the coals. Before long, the water was warm and we could clean ourselves before walking to the bus stop. From the house, it was only another five minutes' walk, and from there, I think, another hour-and-a-half to Queenstown by bus.

The bus terminal in Queenstown was very busy. I felt a bit lost in such a crowded place. Of course, it was nothing like it is today. These days, it is much more crowded than then. But having come from the rural area, I still got a shock at seeing all these people.

We found our way to the main street that led to Jongile's work, a walk that didn't take us very long. My husband was surprised to see us, and his confused look made me laugh a little.

'*Molo, bhuti kaNontombi,*' I greeted him.

As it was only the middle of the morning and many hours before Jongile finished work, Nontombi and I asked him for the key to his room in the location so that we could walk there and wait for him. But Jongile wouldn't hear of it. He insisted on taking us to the location in his motorcar. It was only a short drive, he said, and it would not take him away from work for long.

When we got to the location, he stopped the car in front of one of the larger houses and hooted. Neither Nontombi or I asked him why he did this, but waited patiently until, after a short wait, a smiling Yoliswa came out of the house. When she saw us sitting in the car with Jongile, this smile quickly disappeared.

'*Tyhini! Molweni! Ndothukile andikhange ndanicinga nifuna isitshixo!*' she said, almost falling over her own feet. 'Oh, greetings! I did not expect you. Do you want the key?'

I thought Yoliswa looked nervous as she slipped my husband the key. When she was about to turn back towards the house, I said, 'Why don't you come along with us?'

I don't know what she thought of this, but she nodded her head and joined us in the motorcar. I don't know what Nontombi made of this either, but she said nothing. I looked ahead, out of the window. My mind was racing. *What should I do now? Should I say anything?*

I glanced sideways at Jongile, who steered the motorcar around another corner, his face a mask.

No one spoke.

When we got to his room, Jongile opened the door, lifted Thokozile off my lap to kiss her cheek and cooed to her how much he had missed seeing her. Then he left.

It was a very uncomfortable situation. None us said anything. Nontombi made coffee on the stove while I washed my nipples and started to breastfeed Thokozile. Yoliswa was buzzing around like a fly trapped in a bottle, doing all sorts of things so that she would not have to sit down and talk to me. Now that I think about it, I don't know why she had agreed to come back with us. In the end, she asked after my other baby and my in-laws, all the while packing some clothes into a bag that she picked up from the far corner of the room.

'I am going home now,' she said when I didn't answer her. 'You know, I had that key only because your husband and his cousin asked me to help clean the room and do their washing. But now that you are here, your husband won't need me anymore.'

I looked at her then. I looked her straight in the eye while she spoke, and I *knew* that she was lying. *That is not the truth, and you know it, Yoliswa!* I thought. *You are Majola, as I am, and you are having an affair with my husband. How can you?*

But I said nothing. And she left.

When Jongile came home that evening after work, he asked me why we had come to Queenstown without letting him know. I told him that it was to be a surprise, that I had spoken to his mother about staying with him for a while, and that I did not want Yoliswa there with him without me.

'But why?' my husband asked.

I could not tell him the truth. He would have been so cross with his sister for telling me, so I made up an excuse. I told him I missed my husband, something that I think he was pleased to hear.

'But what can I do if you will not allow Yoliswa to help me with my laundry?' he asked.

'You can take the washing to a laundrette, or a dry cleaner.'

My husband looked closely at me. 'Please, my wife,' he said slowly. 'You do know that there is no other woman who could take your place, don't you? I think about you and our little daughters every day with pride in my heart. You are the only one.'

But I was not so sure.

Nontombi and I stayed with my husband the rest of the week before we all went back home to my in-laws for the weekend in Jongile's motorcar. My husband had made me feel so special during those days in Queenstown, laughing and joking with me and being such a sweet father to my daughter, that I had lost all my suspicions about him and Yoliswa.

Could Nontombi have been wrong? Or did my husband, now we had spent some time together, realise that he didn't really want to be with Yoliswa?

I didn't know, and I didn't ask.

6

Living a lie

Many months went by. Nothing else happened to make me doubt my husband, so I completely forgot about Yoliswa. Life was good with my little daughters, my parents-in-law and Jongile, when he came home on the weekends.

The next time I visited my husband in Queenstown was on a hot day in October. The year was 1961. Jongile had told me that he wanted to spend more time with his daughters, and my in-laws had agreed that I could go to him, but with only one of the children, as they felt that their home would be too empty without both. Lindiwe stayed behind.

Jongile was waiting for us at the bus terminal and was very pleased to see us. I, too, was quite excited to be there. He took us to his motorcar and opened the door for me and Thokozile, making me feel even more special. It was a wonderful feeling to be in the passenger seat next to Jongile. The baby was on my lap and the wind brushed my face through the open window. It was as if I was free from everything. We drove to the location, where my husband and I had some tea before settling down for the evening.

I was very happy during this visit to Queenstown, and felt that my husband and I had never been closer before. *This is good for us*, I thought. *Good for our marriage.* All thoughts of Yoliswa had completely gone. I did not even think about her any more. It was as if she had never even existed.

Until the next time I visited my husband. How foolish I had been! How could I have thought that those feelings of freedom and happiness would last?

Jongile had asked his mother to let me stay with him for a full week, telling her that he had been feeling lonely and wished for his wife to be with him. Thokozile was nearly a year old by now, and no longer on the breast, making it possible for her to stay with Ma.

This time, luckily, I did not have to walk that long distance to the bus station because a cousin of my in-laws, who worked on one of the nearby white-owned farms, was going the same way. He picked me up from my in-laws with his horse-drawn cart early in the morning, dropping me off at the bus station. He asked for a little bit of money for the ride.

Unlike the last time, my husband wasn't at the bus terminal to meet me. So I took my bags and walked the short distance to his office to fetch the key to his room.

Jongile was very pleased to see me and, after apologising for not meeting me at the terminal, he asked after the weather at the Nkonkobe Mountains. He then told me how he had been so busy with his job that even now he could not get away to take me to his room.

So he gave me the key and told me to let myself in.

I didn't mind going to that house by myself. I actually quite liked to be alone, watching the city and everything in it as I walked along those streets. It took me about fifteen minutes to get to the location and my husband's room.

Just as I was about to turn the key, Mama Mamfene, Jongile's landlady, appeared. She was a tall, good-looking, slim person, with skin the colour of dark chocolate and plaited hair. I think she was about seventy or so, but she did not look it. Her hair was as black and shiny as the feathers of a raven.

I had met this lady before on earlier trips to Queenstown and already I was very fond of her. She always showed me much kindness, chatting with me and asking after Lindiwe and my in-laws' home. So when she invited me to come inside her house for a cup of tea with her and her daughter, I was happy to agree.

But my happiness was cut short when I heard why Mama Mamfene wanted to speak with me.

'*Awu, Nowam. Uyayazi la ntombazana uYoliswa le yaye incedisa umyeni wakho?* You know that girl, Yoliswa, who was helping your husband with the household chores?'

Oh, God. What about her? What is she going to tell me about her? It was then that I realised that I hadn't really forgotten about Yoliswa. No, I hadn't forgotten about that woman at all. She had been at the back of my mind all along. Like a ghost. And I realised then that I had been believing a lie. A lie that I had told myself, and did not doubt. A lie I had chosen to live.

I sat and listened quietly as Mama Mamfene told me about the day before, when two men had shown up asking to speak with my husband. They had come together with a young woman. One of these men was that woman's brother, the other her relative. They were there to tell Jongile that the woman was pregnant. That Yoliswa was going to have his child.

Why did I pretend all those months that there was nothing to worry about? Why, why, why? I should have known that something was wrong. That something had been going on between my husband and that girl. And now this woman was pregnant with my husband's child.

I looked into Mama Mamfene's eyes and saw kindness and pity. I felt like crying.

'*Musa ukuzikhathaza,*' I said. 'Don't worry. I will not tell my husband that I spoke with you. Thank you for telling me.'

When Jongile returned from work that evening, he stopped short after kissing me. 'What is wrong, my wife? You don't look very happy this evening.'

I didn't know what to say. I still felt very sore in my heart, but I did not want him to know that I knew about him and that cousin of mine, so I just told him that I was feeling tired.

He believed me. I sat down with him as we talked about his day and about home and Thokozile. He missed both our children during the weeks at work, he said, and always thought about the little things they did. He mimicked Thokozile, and the way she pushed up her eyebrows. We laughed about that, but my laugh felt empty in my chest.

That week went by very slowly. I think it was because I could not stop myself from thinking about Jongile and Yoliswa the whole time while my husband was at his office. But finally, it was coming close to the weekend.

'Why don't we go home this weekend?' Jongile said early on Saturday morning. 'Then we can come back tomorrow evening.'

'Oh, you want to visit your parents and the children and then come back to Queenstown with me?'

'Yes.'

When I look back to those days, I don't know how I managed to live like that, carrying on as though everything was all right and there was no problem at all. But I did.

We were about halfway to the Nkonkobe Mountains when Jongile stopped his motorcar and said, 'My wife, I want you to learn how to drive this car.'

'*Awu, bhuti kaNontombi! Ndiyoyika!* I am scared to drive!'

'There is nothing to fear.'

So I sat behind the steering wheel and listened to what he told me. In those days, there were not many cars on those gravel roads, so I had a long stretch of road to learn in. At first, I was very scared but then, as I grew more bold, I found I really liked driving. I think I was actually quite good at it!

Jongile only took over the wheel again when we drove across farmers' land, because there were many gates to be opened and closed.

My in-laws were very happy to see us, but less happy when they heard their son telling them that he wanted to take me and his daughters back with him to Queenstown.

127

'We don't want to let Lindiwe and Thokozile go,' said my mother-in-law. 'And your wife, Nowam, she must not stay all the time. We need her here to collect wood and fetch water.'

But my husband put his foot down, and in the end they agreed that my daughters and I could stay with my husband for a month. But after that, they said, it would be time for us to come back to them.

On the way back to Queenstown, Jongile gave me another driving lesson, and towards the end of the journey, it was *me* driving that motorcar through all of those gates. I really liked driving, and by the end of that day I felt very confident working those pedals and moving that steering wheel. A few days later, my husband even brought back a book from work that teaches road signs.

'Then you can drive all the time, Nowam!'

It felt so good to be learning something again! It was almost like being back in school. I was thankful to Jongile for his kindness. Maybe things are going to work out with him after all.

But things were about to turn bad once again. About two weeks later, on a Sunday evening just as the sun was setting, my husband and I were laughing and playing with Lindiwe and Thokozile when we heard a knock on the door. It was Yoliswa and her brother. The brother who was a cousin to me.

My cousin's brother looked at me sharply, then turned to my husband and said, 'We are here to speak privately with you, Jongile.'

Jongile stopped me from getting up. 'There are no secrets here,' he said. 'It is only my wife and me here. Speak.'

So this man did. 'My sister is pregnant with your child, and so far you have paid nothing to her parents or to her. Why do you not support your own blood?'

Yoliswa's brother was getting very angry. He was shorter than Jongile, but a tough-looking man. In his anger, his muscles seemed to grow harder. He threw a long stick on the floor of the room with a loud crack.

'If you do not start supporting your child, I will take you to court!'

Jongile was furious. 'How dare you come into my house and say these things in front of my wife and children?' he yelled. 'I *do* give Yoliswa money to buy food for the baby!'

But this man was just as angry as my husband, and he began to shout. 'I will get you, Jongile. You are going to support your child.'

At this, Jongile took Yoliswa's brother by the arm and told them both to get out.

I felt as if someone had hit me in the stomach and all the air had left my body. Shock and confusion were fighting with anger and hatred to rule my heart.

The minute they left the room, Jongile turned to me. 'I am really sorry, Nowam. Please forgive me! Yes, it is true. I did make that girl pregnant. But that does not mean I don't love you! I was just lonely here, on my own. That is why I wanted you with me here all this time.'

He told me that Yoliswa's mother had come to visit him several months ago, saying that she was glad that Yoliswa was helping him because she knew Jongile's parents. She said that she didn't want her daughter to go out and look for another man while my husband was looking after her.

'That is why I had an affair with her. It was an accident,' he said. 'I made her pregnant and I am so sorry.'

I said, 'Do you think her mother was telling you that you could do that to her daughter?'

'Yes,' he replied. 'She said her daughter must not go out and look for another man while I was looking after her.'

You must remember that I was still very young, and this was the father of my children. I trusted every word he said. I even felt sort of relieved, believing that he still loved me. I thought that Jongile had just made a mistake, and that it was Yoliswa and her mother who had tricked him into doing what he had done.

So *that* was why she could not look me in the eye that time I first saw her at the house!

The next day, Monday, Jongile was summonsed to the magistrate's court in Queenstown. There, he was ordered to pay child support to Yoliswa.

My husband never told me how much he paid for that baby. And I never asked. It was not my place even to know how much money he was earning at his job. He gave money to his parents and then, if Ma wanted, she would give me a little to buy soap or things like that.

A few months after the birth of Yoliswa's child, I heard that the child had become ill and had died. I never saw that baby.

And I never saw Yoliswa again.

7

Strange gifts and bad dreams

From that moment on, I began visiting my husband in Queenstown as often as I could. My in-laws had agreed to let me stay more with my husband because they knew that their son would be happier to have his wife with him in town.

I made these visits without my daughters as my parents-in-law wanted the children to stay with them. I knew how fond they were of the girls, so I agreed. It was better this way in any case because the room Jongile was renting was quite small. There was only one three-quarter bed, which my husband and I shared.

During one of these visits to Queenstown, something very strange happened to me. It was a Monday evening in December, and I was feeling so tired that straight after our supper of stewing beef with dumplings, which was my husband's favourite meal, I went to sleep. I think it was only about nine o'clock.

'*Kutheni usoloko usozela nje kule mihla!*' my husband said when I got into bed. 'You are always tired these days, going to bed early and having bad dreams. What's going on?'

I didn't know, but it was true. I could hardly keep my eyes open in the evenings, even though it wasn't very late at all. And then, in the middle of the night, I'd wake up upset after a bad dream.

It was the same that Monday evening. I fell asleep quickly, only to wake up to see that the room was full of people who were staring at me and whispering to each other. Confused, I asked Jongile what was going on. He told me it was five in the morning, and that this was the first time I had woken up since I had gone to sleep the night before.

I needed to have a wee, so I got up and walked out of the room to the public toilet outside, which was only a few steps from the room. When I came back, everyone started to ask me all sorts of questions. What had happened to me, how was I feeling and so on. But my husband stopped them, telling them that I was very tired and needed to go back to sleep instead of answering all their questions.

So I fell asleep again, but only for a short while. When I woke again, all those people were still in the room. '*Jongile, ngobani na aba bantu, bafuna ntoni?* Jongile, who are these people?' I whispered to my husband. 'What do they want?'

I was beginning to feel embarrassed about them all staring at me. I knew only Mama Mamfene and her granddaughter, Nomda. There were three other men that I did not know.

'That gentleman is a witchdoctor, Nowam,' Jongile explained. 'And those other gentlemen are *abakhwetha begqirha,* witchdoctors in training.' He looked at me on the bed. 'A very strange thing happened to you last night. You fell asleep as soon as you put your head down. You didn't even stir when I blew out the lamp and lay down next to you. I, too, fell asleep, but soon I woke up because you were screaming.'

I looked at him. I didn't remember this, not at all.

'Your screams were so loud that Mama Mamfene and her granddaughter came knocking at the door, asking what was wrong with you.'

I got such a shock when he told me this. I still couldn't remember a thing.

'And while you were screaming, I tried to look for matches to light the paraffin lamp but I couldn't find any,' said my husband. 'With all this knocking on the door, I sort of found my way in the dark to let them in.'

My husband looked very upset. Mama Mamfene later told me that Jongile had opened the door without even realising he was wearing only his underpants.

'You screamed so loud, they thought I was beating you,' Jongile said in a grave voice.

With the help of Nomda's torch, they soon found the matches and got the paraffin lamp burning. By then I was quiet and lying very still on the bed. I looked like a dead person, Jongile said.

This gave everybody a huge shock. They tried to wake me up, but no matter how they shook me, I didn't open my eyes. Mama Mamfene even tried slapping my face, but this didn't work either. In the end, they didn't know what to do anymore, so they bent over my still body to listen for my heart. They were very relieved to hear it beating and feel that my body was warm. I was not dead, after all.

I didn't know what to say. I was in a big shock when I heard all this, and my head was thick with the smell of the herbs that the witchdoctor had used to break the sleeping spell. I looked at Jongile and saw concern in his beautiful brown eyes. He cared for me so much!

Jongile then told me that Mama Mamfene had sent for the witchdoctor. That is what we used to call this sort of doctor in those times. Nowadays, most people don't call them that anymore because it sounds a bit strange, as if they are involved in witchcraft. No, today these doctors are called traditional healers or diviners. But this is what we used to call them then.

My grandfather, Mama's father, was a very well known witchdoctor himself when he was a young man. Mbiyozo, that was his name. Mama used to tell us children stories about him and the rest of her family in the evenings, once the dishes had been washed and put away. She never liked dirty dishes to be left for the morning, so we always got those done first before settling down to listen to one of her stories.

One evening, she told us, a group of men arrived at her father's home on horseback to talk to him about the drought. I think that was in the year 1908, or even the year before. It was very dry and the crops and the cattle were suffering. They wanted my grandfather to ask the ancestors what they could do to make it rain.

Mama's father told them that witchcraft had been used, and that a magic spell had been thrown into one of the deep rivers that usually never dried up, no matter how hot it was. The men asked my grandfather to go with them to this deep river where there was still a small natural pool at the bottom, so he put on his *isidla,* rubbed his naked body in wood ash and, carrying only his spear, he ran all the way next to those men on their horses.

Traditionally, Xhosa men did not wear clothes but only this *isidla* or, if the weather was cold, their blankets. This *isidla* covers a man's private parts. It looks sort of like a narrow tube that is made from animal skin and is tied to the waist by a string.

Anyway, my grandfather ran to that river and lifted the spell. When they left that place, the sky suddenly broke and rain was pouring down! He was a very good witchdoctor.

Getting back to that evening of my having a bad dream. Mama Mamfene sent for a lady witchdoctor and, when she came, she said that a spell had been cast on me. A woman had done so, she told Jongile, but she didn't know the name of this person. She, too, could not wake me up.

So they fetched another witchdoctor, again a lady, who used special cards to try and wake me. But that didn't work either. I think this spell must have been very strong for it to work so well on me. The second lady witchdoctor asked Mama Mamfene to come with her outside while Jongile was left to stay with me. There, she told Mama Mamfene that nothing could be done for me. I was dead!

Naturally, this gave Mama Mamfene a huge shock. But neither she nor Jongile believed this, so they then went to find yet another witchdoctor. This third witchdoctor came together with his two *abakhwetha beqgira*, and that is when I finally woke for the first time. But the sleeping spell was still working, and it was only when I went to sleep again that this third witchdoctor could finally break it. I didn't remember anything that happened, not at all.

'*Umfazi wakho lo uyagula, ubulawa yintombi othandana nayo, ifuna afe ukuze yona ifumane wena.* Your wife is ill, she has been placed under a spell by a woman you know,' the witchdoctor said, looking directly at my husband. 'She wants your wife to die so that she can have you!'

'Do you remember what happened in your dream, Nowam?' Jongile asked. I nodded. 'Can you tell us about it?'

'In my dream,' I said, 'I saw a very tall man walking towards me, wearing long khaki trousers. I couldn't see his face. From the waist up he was shrouded in thick mist, so that I could not see his head and upper body. That is what was so scary about him!

'I grew frightened as this tall man came closer. I don't know why. It felt as if he was evil, almost. He took a step towards me, then another step, and another and another and then I started to scream, and that was all.'

'Is this the first time you had such a dream?' the witchdoctor asked. Without waiting for an answer, he carried on, 'My ancestors are telling me that this was not the first time for these bad dreams.' He then turned to Jongile. 'Your girlfriend is bewitching your wife! You must act upon this before it is too late!'

He then waved his hands to show that he was finished and began to take off the many strands of beads from around his waist, wrists and head before he spoke to Jongile again. 'There is a man, Mr Bayi, who is a very fine herbalist. He will help your wife to get rid of the poison inside her body that your girlfriend has had put upon her.'

My husband paid the witchdoctor for helping me and for breaking that bad spell. I don't know how much he paid. He then took them to their homes in his motorcar while Mama Mamfene and her granddaughter stayed to keep me company. Then they, too, left me.

I felt horrible. I knew that Jongile did not believe in witchcraft or *muti,* traditional medicine, and to be honest, neither did I. Not really. But things have happened in my life that leave me wondering. For example, many years later, in 1978, Joyce, a friend of mine, had a teenage daughter who suffered from *iintwala zehagu,* pig lice. This happened long after I had left my home in the eastern Cape Province.

Anyway, I don't really know if it really was pig lice, but it looked just like it. It was nothing like human lice. One morning, Joyce asked me to go with her to a well-known witchdoctor in Gugulethu, outside Cape Town. Joyce, like me, was working as a domestic for a white family. It was a Saturday, and we both had the day off.

We went there together by car – Joyce, her three schoolgirl daughters, me and the person driving the car. The witchdoctor showed us into a room and, while we sat down, he took a hat made of baboon skin off a shelf, put it on his head and – after asking for his fee of about thirty rand – told Joyce that someone had bewitched her daughter.

'This person wants your daughter to be hated by everybody,' he said. 'When your daughter writes her exams, she cannot concentrate because she is scratching all the time because of these lice. This person wants her to fail her school exams.'

The witchdoctor then took us to a herbalist in the location and, after taking the medicine he prescribed, this girl never had those lice again. Her mother was very happy for her daughter, and she passed all her exams.

The second thing that happened to make me believe a little in witchdoctors and their spells happened about a week before I had those bad dreams. I had been in Jongile's room when there was a knock on the door. I opened it to a lady who brought all sorts of things for me, telling me that her friend, Nosipho, had told her that I was staying in Queenstown with Jongile.

I knew who this lady was talking about. Nosipho was the daughter of Mama's good friend, Mama Cidi. I knew her very well.

This strange lady then said that she had just come back from De Aar, a town very far away from us in the Karoo, and that she had brought me all these nice things. She then gave me beefsteak, tomatoes, onions, home-brewed ginger beer and paraffin. I remember feeling surprised, and asked her why she was giving these things to me when she did not even know me.

To this the woman said, '*Awu! Thula wethu!* No! Be quiet, sister! I know you through Nosipho.' She then told me that she got all these things for free from her work, although she had brewed that ginger beer herself.

Well, I did think it was a bit strange, but in those days people still did nice things for each other without them even asking, so that is what I thought she had done. This we called *ububele*, which means kindness.

At the time, my sister Nomi, Ntsodo's twin, was visiting me for two days in Queenstown because I had been sick with flu. She had wanted to come and look after me.

'I don't like that woman, Nomfusi,' she said when the lady left the room. 'I don't know why, but she looks strange. There is something about her that doesn't feel right.' But those groceries looked very nice, so Nomi did cook the meat and fed me some of the stew.

When Jongile came home that evening, he picked up the bottle of home-brewed ginger beer from the table.

'*Ivela phi na le bhotile yejinja*? Where does this bottle come from?'

When I told him, he agreed with Nomi that this was something very strange. 'You can't drink this woman's ginger beer!'

'Why not?'

'Because you don't know her. You don't know who she is, or why she has given you all these things.'

But I was determined and, with my flu, I was very thirsty. I wanted that drink.

'Well, one glass then.'

That evening I went to bed before everyone else, even before Thokozile, who Nomi had brought with her from my parents-in-law to visit me. She was playing all sorts of baby games with my husband and sister.

That night was the first time I had these scary dreams. And they were horrible, horrible, horrible! I was dreaming that I had a very bad stomach ache, suffering so much with pain that it seemed real. In this dream, someone was telling me that it was because of that drink that I was so much in pain.

Right then I woke up, only to find that my tummy was actually very painful. My head was so dizzy that I could not see anything, except for bright lights that were like shooting stars. I felt very hot and feverish as well. When I tried to get up, I fainted.

My husband and Nomi woke up when they heard me fall. While Jongile lit the lamp, Nomi rushed to me. I was already crawling towards the door because my stomach was making grumbling sounds and felt very runny. Before I could get outside, my tummy was already going. It was terrible, but I couldn't stop it. Jongile and my sister looked at each other with shock. They could see that I was very, very sick.

The next thing I remember, Nomi was kneeling down with me and bringing a mug with liquid to my lips. 'Drink this, Nomfusi,' she said. It was full with her warm urine. I hesitated.

'Please, Nomfusi,' she said. 'Drink this quickly. This is our mother's medicine. She always said that if someone is poisoned, you must make them drink urine very quickly.' Mama, of course, was also a herbalist and she knew a lot about curing illnesses. I knew that her remedy would be good.

So I drank my sister's fresh wee. It left me feeling nauseous, which made Jongile very angry. He took that mug and splashed it across the floor of the room. I know that he did not believe in *muti*, and I think that is why he got so annoyed.

But I had already swallowed enough of it for it to work. Soon my body started to cool down. The faintness disappeared and I felt much better.

Nomi left the next day, and a week after that I had the bad dream from which only that third witchdoctor could wake me. I could never explain these stories.

About two weeks after I was healed, Nosipho, Mama Cidi's daughter, came to visit me in Queenstown. I was happy to see my friend, and we could not talk fast enough to tell each other our news. When I told her the story of that lady who had brought those things for me, Nosipho said she knew the woman, and that she had until recently been working in Queenstown as a domestic. Nosipho said this woman left town after Jongile found the place where she was working and had visited her. Apparently, he said he would beat her for bringing those things to me that gave me those bad dreams. After that, this lady disappeared.

I did not understand why she had gone to all that trouble to give me that bad stuff, or how my husband knew who she was or where to find her.

'Didn't you know, Nomfusi?' said Nosipho.

And then I understood.

That woman had been my husband's lover.

Even though Jongile did not believe in these things, he did take me to the herbalist, Mr Bayi, to make me well again. I think he got such a big shock when I didn't wake up that night that he wasn't going to take the risk.

I had known Mr Gubevu Bayi for a long time, from the days when I was a schoolgirl. Although I had met him many times, it was never for medicinal reasons. My husband had never met him before.

Mr Bayi's large black eyes were locked into mine as I told him about my dreams. He scared me a little bit, staring like that, but his wife, Zengele, told me that this was his way and that I would be fine. Her husband, she told me, always used the right herbs.

Mr Bayi was a big man. He was lying on his side on a mat, puffing on his pipe without saying anything as he listened to what I told him. And at the end of my story, Jongile asked him to come back with us to my in-laws so that he could take a few days to make me well again.

He agreed. Packing all sorts of herbs in his medicine bag, he told his wife that he would be back in a few days. We left in my husband's motorcar.

I remember feeling very confused all the way home. The medicine he had already given me was very bitter and it did not taste nice, not at all. But that was not the worst part of it. When we got to my in-laws, he worked on me with many different medicines. What scared me the most was the time he cut me with a razor blade, three small, quick cuts on each side of my wrists and ankles. This was done to drive out the evil spirits from my body and, even though I was terrified, it did work.

For, after Mr Bayi was finished with me, I never had those dreams again.

8
I hoped my husband would change

When Thokozile turned one year old in March of 1962, we celebrated her birthday at my in-laws' home. This was done during the weekend, when Jongile was back from Queenstown. For the celebration, a sheep was slaughtered to make sure that my baby would always want to come home to the place of her ancestors. That was our culture.

I remember sitting with her on my lap while that sheep was brought to us, right to the front door. 'Thokozile, there is your sheep,' said my father-in-law. 'You are now accepted by the ancestors.'

The same had been done for Lindiwe when she turned one year old. When that sheep was brought in front of her, she started pointing at it, making *bah-bah* sounds. Everybody had laughed.

After my father-in-law showed Thokozile her sheep, it was taken away and slaughtered, and the meat was cooked by my family. The faces of both my baby and myself were smeared with *imbola ebomvu,* red ochre. This was the tradition of the traditional Xhosa people, the Amaqaba. Like many other people, my great-grandparents were Amaqaba. The white people sometimes called us the Ochre People.

The Amaqaba also used to dye their blankets and clothes and bodies with red ochre. Apart from these red blankets, which they wore when the weather was cold, their men used to walk around naked. That is, apart from the *isidla,* the material that covers a man's private parts. This paint was made from red earth that we fetched from the river. When water was added, it became a very rich and bright red colour. It was believed that our ancestors very much liked this red ochre and using it was our way to respect them. The word *qaba* means to smear. Today, the word *qaba* also means a person who has never been to school.

While we were sitting there with this paint on our faces, waiting for the meat to be brought to us, Jongile cut a piece of meat from the shoulder of the sheep and I was told to put this piece into Thokozile's mouth. No one was to eat from that shoulder except for me and the baby.

This kind of custom is still going strong with my people, even to this day. Some clans do it by slaughtering a goat. I remember Mama telling me that when the twins, Ntsodo and Nomi, were one year old, she and my father had slaughtered two sheep, one for each of the children. When the twins were about eight or nine years old, Ntsodo started being sick all the time. The witchdoctor said that it was because they had killed two sheep for the twins. 'The Majola ancestors are not happy,' this witchdoctor had said gravely. 'An ox was meant to be slaughtered for these twins.'

By that time, Mama was alone. Her husband, our father, was already dead. So she alone obeyed that witchdoctor and slaughtered an ox, and from that day Ntsodo was well again.

On that happy Saturday when we celebrated Thokozile's first year, a very sad thing happened to bring back all the trouble in my marriage again. I didn't know this then, but now, looking back over those long years, I see that that day was the beginning of the death of the union between Jongile and me.

I was inside our rondavel in the evening, making a fire, when Nontombi came in and whispered, 'Sisi, my boyfriend is outside in the dark, waiting for me. I want to go outside quickly and speak with him, but I don't want my brother to see me with him. He would kill me if he knew.'

I told her that if he asked I would say that I didn't know where she was. She thanked me and quietly slipped out of the room. I think she was about seventeen then, a lovely young girl.

A few moments later, my husband came inside the rondavel, looking very angry. 'What is going on, Nowam?' he demanded. I wondered if I had done something wrong.

'I saw you outside with another man!'

Relieved, I smiled at him and told him that he had made a mistake, that I had not been outside since the sun had set.

The next thing I knew, my husband gave me a *klap* across my face so hard that I fell to the floor. I was so shocked that he had hit me that I didn't know what to do. I couldn't even cry. The next thing I remember was that Ma burst into the room.

'*Yima! Yima!*' she yelled. 'Stop! Stop! Jongile! What are you doing?'

I didn't wait to hear any more and ran out of the room into the darkness. Behind me, I heard Thokozile begin to cry at the noise and my husband pick her up and whisper to her to go back to sleep.

The funny thing is that I was not really angry or scared as much as I was embarrassed. I ran to the main rondavel, where my in-laws slept.

When Ma found me there, she said, 'That boy is very silly. He doesn't mean to be a bad husband, Nowam. But you must remember to always cry very loudly if he does beat you, so that we can come and stop him. Because if you don't cry, he will keep on beating you. If you cry, he will stop.'

My father-in-law was very angry with my husband. He told his youngest son, who was about twelve years old at the time, to go and fetch Jongile. When my husband finally came, he said he was sorry, and he really did look as though he meant it.

The next morning, I went to the main rondavel to make my in-laws breakfast while Nontombi brought morning coffee to my husband in our room. When we finished our chores, we walked to the river together to fetch some clear spring water to wash the dishes.

'Did you tell your brother that it was you he saw with your boyfriend?' I asked her. I wasn't angry with Nontombi, not at all. I liked her too much for that, and I knew that it wasn't her fault. But I did want to know if she had told her brother.

'*Hayi! Ndiyamoyika ubhuti,*' she said. 'No! I am scared of my brother. But I did tell him that you, Sisi, have got nothing to do with him.'

Luckily, Ma knew the truth about Nontombi's boyfriend. It sort of helped that she knew I had nothing to be sorry for. But I don't think she told my husband about that boy either.

That was the first time Jongile beat me. I didn't take it badly. I just thought that he was jealous, and that that was because he loved me. Strangely enough, it even made me feel a little proud. Because it meant that my husband really loved me, after all.

9

About my cousin who went to jail

Apartheid wasn't something I was aware of much during those days in the rural east of the Cape Province. But sometimes news of trouble did reach us and, when it did, I began to see that there were a lot of problems in our country. I didn't know how bad things were, though, or what was happening to the black people of South Africa.

I also knew nothing about a great man, Nelson Rolihlahla Mandela, who was born in the Transkei. Only much later did I learn about him, just like I was to learn of other important leaders. Mr Govan Mbeki, Mr Robert Sobukwe, Mr Steve Biko, leaders whose ideals for our people would eventually change all these apartheid things.

The first time these problems touched my home was when my cousin Rolo was sent to jail. This was in 1963. The same year, I learnt later, Mr Mandela was charged with sabotage and trying to overthrow the white government. But I didn't know that at the time, of course. I only heard it much later.

This cousin of mine was the lastborn son of my father's brother. Some time before, he had gone to Cape Town to join the Pan Africanist Congress, the PAC. In those days it was not legal to be part of the PAC or the ANC. What's more, African people were not allowed to work or live in Cape Town without a Pass. Rolo was with the PAC and he did not have a Pass. So the police had two reasons to look for my cousin.

When we heard that the police were looking for Rolo, Mama and I went to visit my cousin's mother and his young wife in Rwantsana, a rural community near Lady Frere, east of Queenstown.

Leaving the girls with my mother-in-law, I walked all the way to Mama's home. From there, we took a bus to Queenstown and, from there, another to Rwantsana. In all, it was a very long way to travel. I can still see myself sitting in that big bus, a bit frightened as it drove fast along those gravel roads that were full of bumps and holes. We were going very close to the edge of a cliff, and, when I looked down, I saw a long drop below me. Far down was a river so wide that it seemed to go on forever. So I closed my eyes and did not look down again.

When we finally got to the home of my aunt, she told us that her son had been taken away by the police. This had happened a few days before. Mama and I listened with shock as my aunt told us about how these policemen burst into her home, asking where her son was. If she and her husband didn't tell the police where he was, they said, they would be put in jail. The police then confiscated a gallon of petrol, saying that my cousin was planning to use it for a petrol bomb. This, we learnt later, was not true. The petrol, my cousin said, was just to operate his tractor.

Well, my aunt and her husband couldn't tell the police where Rolo was because they really didn't know. As it turned out, Rolo and two of his PAC friends from Cape Town had been hiding in the nearby Engqoko Mountains, hoping that they would be safer there. But news spread very fast of the police giving Rolo's parents trouble, and a few days later my cousin and his friends came down the mountain to hand themselves in at the police station at Lady Frere. They did not want their families to suffer while they were safe in the mountains.

My cousin and his comrades were found guilty of sabotage in the Queenstown magistrate's court and each given ten years and six months in prison. Mama and I were feeling very sorry for our family. I couldn't imagine anyone being locked away in prison for all those years.

It was then, seeing how unfairly my cousin was being treated and how brave he was in that court, that I started wanting to know about the politics of my country. And the more I learnt, the more proud I became that my cousin was one of those who was fighting for freedom for all of us.

The last six months of Rolo's sentence were later pardoned. The first three months he served in East London. After that, he was sent with a few others to Robben Island. I think that was around Christmas time, but I don't remember if it was before or after Christmas. I think it was still 1963.

Over the years, my cousin saw many people on that island. Other prisoners who shared his 'crime' – to set free South Africa and her people.

He was there at the same time as Mr Mandela, and only recently did he tell me that he had actually seen Tata Madiba there, just across from him, on the other side of one of the prison fences.

When Rolo went to jail, I felt very sorry for my cousin's young wife and his two baby sons. She had such a brave heart, and it broke mine to see her without her husband. Those little boys were only three years and one month old when he was sent away. Being a young mother of two children myself, I knew how hard that must have been for her to be there with those children, without a husband.

The day after Rolo was sent to jail, that young wife and I went to fetch firewood together. She told me then that she was going to wait for her husband. She said that she had got a huge shock when she heard how long his sentence was going to be, but she loved her husband enough to honour him by waiting.

I felt a great admiration for her, and perhaps only now can I really understand how very hard it must have been for that young family. For so many families. But what makes me very happy is that, after all this time, my cousin and his wife are still together. They did not let him out one day before ten years, but when they did she was there. My cousin and his wife were again united in marriage, and, many years after that, they were still together when South Africa became a true democracy.

So it was around this time that I first became aware of what was happening in my country. I saw how unfair some things were, and I saw that there were other things that I did not understand. And, as the years went on, I saw how things got worse.

We started hearing about how those black people who told the police what their own brothers were doing to fight apartheid were punished in a terrible way. Because the people could not forgive their own African brothers for betraying them to the white police.

They called this terrible punishment 'necklacing'. It happened quite often, especially in the cities and big locations, but luckily I never saw it. In a necklacing, a big mob of people would drag a betrayer out of his house and place a tyre around his neck. This tyre was then filled with petrol and set alight. While that person was screaming and yelling, the crowd would watch while he died like that. It seems impossible that people could do this thing to each other, but that is what happened in those days. That is what happened to our African brothers who were informants.

How innocent I was before I knew all this. How innocent we had all been.

I could never have thought then that I would end up in trouble myself, that I would be arrested for breaking the Pass laws. And that I, too, would be put in jail. But all of that happened much later. After I had been in Somerset West for many years.

These stories make me think of another very sad thing that happened to my family because of apartheid. It happened in March 1986, and even today, when I am reminded of what happened, I feel so much grief that I don't think I can bear it.

For that was the day that my nephew, Davide Manyali, died for his country.

Davide was the only son of my brother Ntsodo and his wife, Mambele. He was only twenty-four years old on the day he died, just one month short of his twenty-fifth birthday. I still mourn for him.

Davide was very much involved in the struggle against apartheid. His parents often used to warn him about the many dangers that he chose to face because of his beliefs. But he was a very brave young man, and he always replied, 'Mama, Tata, please do not worry about me. If I die, my blood will sprinkle the tree of freedom. I am happy to die, fighting for freedom.'

This, he did.

The week before he was killed, I remember Mambele telling me of a very strange dream she had had. She had dreamt that she was being chased by lots of people carrying all sorts of guns. In this dream she was running, jumping in the river to hide from those people. Then she heard a gunshot, and realised that she had been shot in the head. She woke up trembling.

She couldn't stop thinking about that dream all week, trying to understand what it meant. She knew it meant something was not good at all.

Davide was not living with his parents at the time. No, he was staying in Gugulethu, to be near to his comrades from the UDF, the United Democratic Front. Even then he didn't stay in one place. He was always moving around because he was so involved in the struggle.

Davide had a wife and two children, a girl of three also called Lindiwe, and Mlamleli, a boy of two years of age. They didn't see their father much. He didn't want to put them in danger, so he didn't live with them.

149

On that very bad day, Davide's mother went with her friend to a funeral in Gugulethu. After the funeral, she and her friend went to the bus station to catch a bus home to Mfuleni township. At the station, a group of people were talking loudly. From them, Davide's mother heard that somebody had been shot close by. The person lay there, dead, covered by a UDF t-shirt.

Soon after Mambele arrived back home, her brother and cousin showed up at her house. They had just come from Gugulethu to bring her very sad news. The body that had lain there, covered by that UDF t-shirt, was the body of her son. He had been shot in the head. Mambele's cousin suspected that Davide may have been killed by the security police. This was because of the thick silence around his death. No one saw or heard anything, even though it was a busy Saturday afternoon and he was shot so close to the station.

When she heard that her only son had been killed, my sister-in-law fainted. She fell right there, on the floor.

When I heard this terrible news, I took the bus from Somerset West to Mfuleni to be with my brother and his wife. Mambele looked much thinner than before, and hardly said a word. She said she did not know where to begin showing her grief for her firstborn and only son. For her Davide.

A few weeks before Davide was killed, he had asked his parents to make sure that his children got an education if something happened to him. He strongly believed that education was the only way for the young children of this country to have better lives.

And so my beloved nephew Davide, who had gone to the funeral of a friend just the previous Friday evening, was dead a few hours later. And one week after that, his father, mother, family and friends went to mourn him. When his mother and my brother went to identify the body on Monday morning, they almost didn't recognise him.

There were many people at the funeral. I remember not

being able to keep from crying when I saw those young men carrying his coffin over their shoulders towards his newly dug grave. '*Senzeni na, senzeni na?*' they were singing. 'What have we done, what have we done?'

The police were there too, carrying rifles. They were keeping a close eye on the ceremony from the top of a water tank, looking out for signs of trouble.

Then the preacher prayed. '*Khumbula, Yehova okusihleleyo.* Remember, Oh Lord, what has happened to us. Look at us, and see our disgrace. Our land is in the hands of strangers. Foreigners are living in our homes. Our fathers have been killed by the enemy, and now our mothers are widows. We must pay for the water we drink; we must buy the wood we need for fuel. Driven hard like donkeys or camels, we are tired, but allowed no rest. To get enough food to stay alive, we went begging to Egypt and Assyria. Amen.'

They never found Davide's murderers.

10

The beginning of the end

But I must go back and tell you about the time when I was still in Queenstown with my husband. And why I finally left him and my children.

After this whole business with Nontombi and her boyfriend and my husband beating me, we went back to being a happy family again, my husband, our two beautiful daughters and myself. I didn't visit Jongile in Queenstown so often anymore, but for a while he came home every weekend to visit us, as he had done before we were married in church.

Then it all changed again. I remember it very well. There had been times before when I felt my relationship with my husband was not going well, and many times when I thought my marriage was going to end. But this time, it really was the beginning of the end.

It was a hot day in early summer when Ma said that she wanted to go to Queenstown to visit my husband. 'Our son has not come home for a whole month, and our groceries are almost finished now,' she said. 'I am going to find out what is happening.'

It was true. My husband had not come home for many weeks. I, too, was wondering why he stayed there in Queenstown instead of joining his wife and family at the weekends.

By this time, we had moved away from the farm in the Nkonkobe Mountains and were living in Tsitsikamma. I think there was some trouble between my father-in-law and the white farmer on that first farm, so we moved away from there. This new place was not far from Nkonkobe and much closer to that bus stop to Queenstown, making it a lot easier to visit Jongile in town.

'*Kulungile mfazi ungaya kunyana wethu asithengele ukutya,*' my father-in-law said to his wife. 'Very well, my wife, you can go and ask our son to buy us groceries.'

The next day, a Monday, Ma woke early and dressed herself smartly to go to Queenstown. She was wearing a dark blue-and-white print skirt that she had made herself with a white blouse, flat black shoes, black *doek* around her head and a shawl around her shoulders. She looked very beautiful. She took her handbag and walked the fifteen minutes to the bus stop while I stayed behind with the rest of the family.

A week passed, and then another, and still Ma had not returned. By the third week, my father-in-law said to Boniwe, 'This is the third week and there is still no sign of your mother! If she has not come back by this coming weekend, you will have to go and find out what is keeping her from coming home.'

That following Monday, Boniwe took the bus to look for Ma. We were all wondering why she had been staying so long, but had to wait for an answer until they all returned the next Sunday.

It was already dark when the faint headlights of a motorcar shone through the open door of the rondavel where we were all sitting and onto the mud wall inside. We had left the top part of the door open to allow the evening breeze to come in and cool us down.

When we saw those lights, we knew that it was Jongile's motorcar, bringing Ma and Boniwe back home. In those days, my husband was one of only a few men we knew who owned a car.

There was no road leading to the rondavel, so Jongile drove through the open veld after leaving the main gravel road from Queenstown. But this evening, he did not stop his car in front of the rondavel. Instead, he drove that motorcar straight past my in-laws' home and parked it close to their cattle kraal.

I remember thinking this was strange. Ma and Boniwe had many groceries to bring in. Why did my husband park his car so far away from the rondavel? *Why?*

Now, of course, I understand very well why. Because he knew that there I, his wife, could not come out to see him. This was because it was believed that the cattle kraal was the place where the ancestors dwelled. As a *makoti*, I was not allowed to go near that kraal, not even if a family member went with me. My sisters-in-law could go there, and I could go to my parents' kraal, but not the other way around. That was the custom.

So my husband parked at the kraal. Because he did not want me to see the other woman in his car.

I was busy making supper when that car arrived, which that evening was home-baked bread with spinach and boiled potatoes. But Jongile did not stay for supper, and at the time I couldn't understand why. He just brought in those groceries, followed by Ma and Boniwe, and, after quickly saying hello to me and the children, left again in his motorcar. He said that he couldn't stay for the night.

He brought us a lot of stuff that evening. Jam and coffee and *amasi* and bread and all sorts of things, which put us all in a very good mood. My father-in-law was happy to see his wife and daughter back home again. He was laughing and chatting all the time during supper. But not me. I knew that something was not right.

The following morning, Mangxabani, my father-in-law's sister-in-law, took me to where the others were not listening and told me that the bread and jam and things had been a gift to my in-laws by a woman who, she said, was my husband's new girlfriend.

She told me that this woman's name was Thulethu, and that she came from St Marks, a rural area about sixty-five kilometres away from Queenstown. Apparently she was divorced from her husband and had six children. This woman had come to Queenstown to look for work and got a job as a cleaner in the Frontier Hospital. I do not know where her children were while she was working, but they were not living with her. Or at least this is what Mangxabani said. It seemed that this lady, Thulethu, was much older than me.

I cannot describe how I felt when Mangxabani was telling me all this. I did not know if I should believe her. Another girl-friend? Again?

I knew then that my husband would never change, but as it wasn't my place to show what I knew, or ask Ma if this was true, I just made a vow to myself that I would not say anything. And I was definitely not going to eat this woman's bread!

That evening, while I dished up supper for us, Ma said, 'I have brought some bread with jam and sour milk, Nowam. You can have some if you like. I know you like sour milk and jam.'

'No, Ma,' I said softly. 'I am going to have some of this home-baked bread. I don't need sour milk, thank you.'

This offended my mother-in-law very much, and the next thing I knew she began to shout at me.

'How dare you turn down the food I offer you!' she yelled. 'Who do you think you are? I struggle to feed my children with whatever I can get my hands on and you dare say no to this good bread?'

I had never seen my mother-in-law so angry before.

'Tell me, Ma,' I said. 'Where does this jam-smeared bread and sour milk come from?'

At this my mother-in-law exploded with rage.

'My son is not some castrated ox!' she shouted. 'He is a man! Marrying you does not mean he is tied to you! That ring around your finger, what do you think that is? It is nothing! A worthless wire. It doesn't mean a thing! My son has a very good girlfriend in that lady in Queenstown. She is a much better person than you. At least she gives me everything I need. She buys me clothes and she puts food on the table for my children. What do you do?'

She kept screaming at me with words that were so bad that I am too embarrassed to speak them again. I was so shocked that she could say all these horrible things. My throat felt sore and my mind went blank. Empty. What could I say? What could I do? I was so hurt. I had done nothing wrong. But then I felt something come up from deep inside me. Something that had been there for a long time.

Anger.

'What do I do?' I yelled back at her. 'What do I do? I wash, I clean, I cook, I do everything for your family!'

That was the first time I ever answered back to her. I had always had great respect for my mother- and father-in-law. Mama had taught me that, to always respect my elders. And, when I left my home as a young *makoti*, my family repeated the lesson, that I must always respect my in-laws and remember my place in my new home.

But this day I could not. I had had enough.

So I told Ma that I had a home, a real home, and a mother, and that she had never given me either of these things. It was a terrible evening, with lots more shouting and crying. Through it all, I never looked at any of the others, at my father-in-law, Nontombi, Boniwe or the youngest son. No. This was between Ma and me.

My father-in-law, who was a gentle and respectful person, tried to break up our fight, but he could not. Ma and I were both too angry.

Later, when I went to bed, I could not fall asleep. I was just lying there, on the bed, crying. But I knew that the moment had finally come. I was going home.

The next morning, Tuesday, my in-laws went to a wedding in one of the neighbouring houses. I did not speak with them that morning, even though I had made them breakfast as usual. Still feeling hurt, I took the children and some of their dirty clothes to the flat rock where I used to do the washing. There was a shallow basin in that rock and, after the rain, the water on that rock was beautifully clear.

Apart from the ache in my heart, it was a wonderful day. The rain had come a few nights earlier, and now the sun was making the green grass sparkle with freshness.

Thokozile was looking at little things on the ground, rocks and insects and twigs, while I was soaping the clothes and rinsing them with that cool, clear water. Lindiwe was further off, playing with some children that lived in the area. I could see her from where I was washing the clothes.

Just then Boniwe came up to me.

'Sisi,' she said, 'I can understand that you are wanting to leave us and go home after that terrible fight with my mother, but please, don't go. Why don't you go to my brother? He is your husband, after all. Talk to him about all this.'

I shrugged my shoulders. Boniwe took a deep breath. 'I must tell you the whole truth, Sisi Nowam.'

That is when I found out. *Pregnant?* This woman, Thulethu, was living together with my husband in Queenstown? No! It can't be. But it was true.

'She buys my mother everything she wants, and they always talk about you,' Boniwe continued. 'When I was there I could see that the moment my brother leaves for work, she is talking to my mother about you. And I heard my mother say that she wants you to go, that she wants Thulethu as her daughter-in-law.'

My blood ran cold.

'They were talking about going to a herbalist, Sisi, and having him give them medicine to make you go away so that Jongile can marry that lady.' Boniwe stopped, as if too embarrassed to carry on. 'My mother said that they could go to her uncle, who is a herbalist, and get medicine so that you will go home and not come back. But that other lady, Thulethu, she said that she wants to get medicine so that you will be struck by lightning.'

In those days, that is what people said when they wanted you dead. They would go to a herbalist or witchdoctor or whatever you want to call it and get special *muti* so that you would be struck dead by lightning.

I didn't know what to think when Boniwe told me this. Witchcraft to make me go away? To kill me?

But Boniwe quickly shushed me. 'No, no, no, Sisi. My mother doesn't want that to happen! She told Thulethu that that is not what she wants, and that she will not allow her to do that. But please, Sisi, don't tell her that you know.'

I promised her and thanked her for telling me the truth, but also told her that I was not going to my husband. I was going home.

I packed a few things and left before my in-laws came back from the wedding that day, with Boniwe begging me the whole time not to go.

'Your husband loves you, Sisi Nowam.'

'Well,' I said to her, 'he has made a second woman pregnant with his child, so I do not see any love there.'

And so I left. For home, and Mama. Once again.

11
The day Jongile 'died'

Mama got a big shock when she saw me walking towards her with Lindiwe beside me, Thokozile strapped to my back, and a big suitcase balanced on my head. But, as always, my home was my home and we were welcomed.

Two days later, Jongile came to Hukuwa to see if I was there. Unlike the other times, my uncle was not happy to see him and wouldn't allow him to speak with me. 'Your mother should come and fetch your wife herself because she is the one who used such bad words when she had a fight with your wife,' he said to Jongile. 'My niece is not a football for your parents to kick around when they please. We do not want you here, Jongile. If you want your wife back, you must tell your mother to come here herself.'

But she never came. We were later told by one of my aunts that my mother-in-law had invited Thulethu to stay with them, so that Ma could deliver Thulethu's baby at their home. My husband's child from another woman.

I know that I should not have gone back to Jongile after that. Maybe if I hadn't, my life would have turned out better. But, when I heard the news that this woman was going to have her baby at my in-laws, I could not just sit and do nothing. I didn't like leaving it like that, not at all. So I decided to go to Jongile in Queenstown, while Thulethu was at his parents' home. I felt that we needed to resolve this quarrelling. For the children, for me. For all of us. But, before I left, I did make one vow.

If my husband and I can patch things up, we will live as a married couple from now on, together in Queenstown, I told myself. *I am never going to live at his parents' home again. Never, never, never again!*

So I went back to Jongile, staying in his new room in Queenstown. After my illness Jongile had moved to a new landlady, a retired schoolteacher who owned a big house some distance away from Mama Mamfene's place. I had left Lindiwe and Thokozile with Mama for a while because I first wanted to find out if Jongile and I really could make up. I asked my husband if he wanted to make Thulethu his second wife, but he said no, that was not what he wanted. He said it was his mother who had asked Thulethu to have her baby at his home. Not him.

It was a strange situation, this. Now I was the one who was staying in that room in Queenstown with Jongile, while Thulethu was at my in-laws.

It was a difficult time, but slowly my husband and I were working out our problems and talking. I was still hoping that soon we would all be living together as a family again. I ignored the fact that this other woman was staying at his parents' home. Looking back, I don't know how I could have lived like that, even for a short time. There I was, staying in Queenstown at the weekends while my husband drove back to his home on Saturday mornings, as he had done when I stayed with his parents. So while they were all together on those two days, I was alone. In Queenstown.

After about two weeks, I went home to Mama to fetch Lindiwe and Thokozile, and shortly after this time I fell pregnant with my third child, Bukelwa, another girl. But I did not know that at the time, of course.

A short time after, I heard that my husband's brother, Keke, had met a girl whom he had taken as his *makoti*. Jongile thought that she would be a good wife for him and Thulethu, who knew this girl very well and was very good friends with her, agreed. But Keke didn't really like her that much. She was fat and had huge breasts, and she was much older than him. She had also had a child from another man before, when she was still living with her parents.

Thulethu and this girl did everything together, cooking and fetching water, and making wood fires and all those sorts of things. They must have had a wonderful time there together at my in-laws. At my husband's home.

But their friendship did not last. To my surprise, a few weeks later, Jongile returned from his home on Sunday evening with this same brother, Keke, who said that he was going to Johannesburg to look for work.

'I don't like what my brother has done,' he told me when Jongile stepped outside. He was talking about Thulethu, of course. 'I don't like that he took this woman to live at our home while you, his wife, are here in Queenstown.'

Keke then explained why he had left his home and was going to Johannesburg to look for a job. Over the weeks, he explained, Thulethu had become very jealous of this other *makoti*, believing that there was something going on between her and Jongile. In the end, those two women got into such a bad fight that my husband had to physically pull them apart. All this made him so angry that he lost his temper with both of them. Before those two women knew what was going on, Jongile whipped them both all over their bodies with a piece of thick wire.

In Xhosa tradition, a man is not allowed to lay a hand on his sister-in-law, so this was very bad. When Keke heard what had happened, he did not want this girl anymore. He could not forget that his brother had beaten his wife, and he did not trust her. I think he also knew that Thulethu probably had good reason to be jealous.

And me? I was starting to not care about any of it anymore. I did not feel jealous or anything like that. No, I was getting on with other things. I had found myself a job in Queenstown as a cleaner and a waitress in a hotel. Actually, I was filling in for a cousin of my husband who went on holiday.

Well, I really liked that job! The hotel was called the Grade Inn, and it was a nice place. Not too grand, but big, clean and comfortable. And Jongile did not mind my working there. I think he was actually happy that I had something to do, and that I was earning a bit of money. I worked at this hotel for about a month and, when that cousin of my husband came back, the hotel manager said that he liked me and that I could stay in that job. I was very happy about that.

I stayed in that job at the Grade Inn for most of the months that I was pregnant. I only stopped working a short time before the birth of the baby. Again, Ma delivered the child at her home. The birth of this girl was more difficult as she was a very big baby.

I did not see Thulethu while I was at Ma's home and, a few weeks after the birth, I went back to work. I worked from about nine in the morning to six in the afternoon. During this time, Ngeduye, my sister Nomi's daughter, looked after the baby as well as the two older girls. This Ngeduye, she was a very sweet girl.

And so our family grew. And even though there was another woman living with my in-laws, I really thought that, this time, my marriage was going to work.

During one of my off days from work, something very scary happened to me. It was a very cold and wet day, and I had just lit the paraffin stove to try and warm up the room. Little Bukelwa was tucked inside a thick, warm shawl and was sleeping on the bed while I had been making *vetkoek* for me and Ngeduye and the girls.

I was just cooking some water on the stove to wash the pots when suddenly the door to the room flew open and a strange lady came in, holding a young child. She was followed by my sister-in-law, Nokhaya, who was Nontombi and Boniwe's older sister. Then came Ma and Nontombi's mother-in-law. I started to worry. What were they all doing here?

They all greeted me, except for Nokhaya and the strange woman, but no one told me why they were there. The woman and her baby sat down on a mat next to the bed. The others sat down on chairs.

It was only much later that I heard why they had come to Queenstown that day. My father-in-law had received a telegram that morning, which his boss had delivered, saying that Jongile had died in a motorcar accident. My in-laws had got such a shock at the news that my father-in-law's boss offered to take them to Queenstown in his bakkie. By this time, my in-laws had moved back to the Nkonkobe Mountains again, where my father-in-law was working for another white farmer.

The person who had sent this telegram about Jongile's 'death' had made a mistake, of course, because my husband was alive and well. But his family didn't know that then.

While they all sat down on the mats in the room, Nokhaya stepped towards the stove and, without even asking me, put her hand in the pot and took out a handful of the *vetkoek* I had been making. She then took the other pot of water off the stove and, turning to the woman and her baby on the mat, she said, 'Oh, my brother's child. You must be hungry.' She then began to make that child food in my pot.

Then I knew. That woman! She was Thulethu!

In a daze, I heard the voice of my father-in-law outside, talking to my landlady. I tried to get myself together and greet everyone in my room and I said the first thing that came to my head. 'Hello, Ma. How are you?'

'We are fine, Nowam,' my mother-in-law replied. 'When are we going to get some tea?'

'Ma, I have only one Primus stove and Sisi Nokhaya is busy with it,' I said. 'And she has just pushed my pot of water aside without asking me.'

When Nokhaya heard me saying this, she turned around and began screaming at me. All this shouting woke Bukelwa up and she began to cry. I picked her up to comfort her and, when she had calmed down a bit, I gave her to Ngeduye. I could see that this was going to be a very nasty quarrel. This sister had never liked me, not from the time when Jongile first brought me to his home, and she was very good friends with Thulethu.

'There!' Nokhaya pointed. 'There is my brother's child! And I am making food for him!'

We were still shouting at each other when Jongile came in. 'What is going on here?'

'It is Nowam,' said my mother-in-law. 'She doesn't want to stop arguing!'

Before I could defend myself, Jongile hit me. Just like that, in front of his family and daughters. He never asked me what had happened, or why we were fighting. He just grabbed me by the back of my neck and threw me across the floor, kicking me in the stomach when I was down.

I started to cry. 'It wasn't me! It wasn't me! Nokhaya started it!'

But Jongile could not be swayed. 'I heard *you*, Nowam! Not my sister. You were the one I heard screaming and shouting!'

Nokhaya said nothing.

Then my father-in-law, who was still outside talking to Jongile's landlady, rushed into the room. 'Stop it, Jongile! You cannot beat your wife like that!'

I got up from the floor and ran as fast as I could from the room. I did not want to stay there another second. I ran straight to the house of Mr Zwelibanzi, a kind man who owned a small shop close to where Jongile and I had stayed before. He shared the same clan as me, Majola, and each time I bought something from his shop, we'd end up chatting.

He was very angry with my husband when I told him my story and gave Jongile a mouthful when he showed up at his place. Jongile knew that I had gone there.

'Why did you hit your wife like that?' Mr Zwelibanzi demanded. 'Instead of just asking her what had happened?'

Jongile told him that he had lost his temper when he had heard all the screaming between me and his sister.

'Well, I am taking your wife and daughters away from you. She is going home to her mother.'

Jongile was not happy to hear this, not at all. He became quiet and even humble. He really did not want me to go, he told Mr Zwelibanzi. He had not meant to hurt me and was sorry it had happened. He had just lost his temper.

My husband looked so sorry that I forgave him. After all, he didn't know what was going on before he came into that room. And I knew he hadn't meant to harm me. So I decided to stay.

By the time we got back, everyone had gone. When my in-laws realised that Jongile was not dead after all, and that he had never been in a car accident, they went back to the bus station where they waited for my father-in-law's employer to take them home in his bakkie. They were gone, and it was as if none of it had ever happened.

It was a situation that had gotten out of hand, and having Thulethu there didn't help. Even after he hit me, I still felt that I had to try again with my husband. It had just been a misunderstanding, and I wanted everything to be all right. I had my children, who were part of my life with my husband. And in those days, a *makoti* was expected to obey her husband without question.

I also felt that part of the fault lay with me. In our culture, there is nothing unusual or wrong to have more than one wife. It was my character, my problem, that I didn't like to share my husband with any woman. And that I couldn't change.

12

Thulethu's child

One evening after work, I came home to find a warm pot on the stove. When I lifted the lid, I found a cooked meal of stamped mealies and beans. The kettle also felt warm, as if it had just boiled. Even the room was warm and comfortable, not at all cold even though winter was still in the air. Had the heater been on? *But how can this be?* I wondered. *Jongile isn't even home from work yet.*

I knew that it could not have been Ngeduye because she was not able to look after the three children that day. I had asked someone else to take care of Lindiwe, Thokozile and Bukelwa, and was about to fetch them from her after coming home.

When I went into the bedroom, I noticed that there was a spot on the bed that was completely wet. *What is this?*

The mystery remained for a few days until Jongile brought up the subject one evening. 'I have something to tell you, Nowam.'

Oh God, what has happened now?

And then he told me. That woman, Thulethu, had left my parents-in-law two weeks earlier with her baby. She had brought my husband's child to Queenstown.

Jongile did not say why Thulethu left my in-laws, or what her plans were. But it explained a lot. Jongile's new landlady later told me that she had seen this woman and her baby going into the room every day as soon as I left in the morning to go to work. She would leave only shortly before I got home.

But now, Jongile told me, Thulethu had left. She had taken the six o'clock train to Johannesburg, where she was going to look for a job. And she had left her child behind.

I later heard from one of my husband's cousins that Thulethu had told him that she could not bear to see Jongile with another woman. Isn't that funny? Because by that time my husband had found himself yet another girlfriend. And this one had also become pregnant.

'His whole family have lied to me,' Thulethu had wailed to Jongile's cousin. 'They all promised me that Jongile was going to divorce his wife and marry me! They had even slaughtered a sheep for my baby. Proof that I was his wife also.'

I knew all this wasn't the child's fault, but I did not want to have anything to do with Thulethu's baby. It was Jongile's child, and he had to deal with it. All I knew was that it was a boy of five months, and that he looked very much like my husband.

'I will take him to my parents this weekend, Nowam,' Jongile said. 'My cousin will come to hold the boy in the car, and then we will leave.'

I could hardly look at this child, but when I did I saw that he was not sitting or even crawling. He was just lying there. This was very strange. At five months? Why was this child not doing any of these things?

'Why don't you come along, Nowam?' Jongile asked me that Friday evening. 'The girls haven't seen their grandparents for a while and I think it will be a good time.'

At least this woman Thulethu has gone, I thought. *Maybe we should go.* It would be the first time I had gone to my in-laws' home since I gave birth to Bukelwa and the whole business of Thulethu, and I knew that Lindiwe and Thokozile would very much like to see their grandparents. They loved them very much. And Jongile's parents would also want to spend time with their new grandchild.

So we went along.

Ma was very happy to see me. I was very surprised. '*Awu! Ndiyavuya ukukubona molokazana. Imkile laa nkunkumakazi ekugqibeleni.* Oh! I am so happy to see you, my daughter-in-law. That rubbish woman has gone at last.'

I didn't know whether to laugh or be insulted. 'That rubbish woman' was, of course, Thulethu. The woman she had wished to be her daughter-in-law instead of me. But now she was greeting me as if we had never fought at all, laughing and hugging Lindiwe and Thokozile all the while. She didn't ever want them to leave again, she said, and when I saw how happy the children were to see their grandparents, it made me feel sad about all the things that had happened.

At that moment, I decided to forgive my mother-in-law for everything and try to be a good *makoti*, and help them whenever they needed me.

Stupid me.

'Why don't we leave the older girls here, with my parents?' Jongile suggested that Sunday afternoon as we were getting ready to leave. 'Then you don't have to worry about who is looking after them when you go to work. And they love to be here.'

It made sense. Ma and my father-in-law were looking very happy at this idea, and the children too. So I agreed. About an hour later, with Bukelwa on my lap, we waved goodbye to my in-laws and the two girls. Within seconds all I could see of where they had been was a great cloud of dust.

About seven months later – it would have been about autumn of 1965 – I went to visit Jongile's parents during the week to help them with things around the farm. That place in Nkonkobe was always very cold in the winter, so I wanted to help them get a lot of firewood before the first snow fell on the mountains.

I had left my job at the Grade Inn a few months before for a job that paid better, as a cleaner at the Sanlam offices in Queenstown. But that week I was on leave.

Ma and the girls were very happy to see me, and we had a nice supper together that night. We were all chatting, chatting, chatting so much! It was good to see Boniwe again, too. I had not spoken with her for a long time. By that time, Nontombi was married and living with her husband, so she was not there.

While we were eating supper, I saw Thulethu's child lying on a mat, as helpless and strangely quiet as the last time I saw him. By now this child was about a year old, and still he was not sitting or crawling. He also never looked you straight in the eye. It was a very strange thing. His eyes would look sideways, a bit like a chameleon.

I had begun to feel very sorry for this child. What was wrong with him? Ma also knew that something was not right and kept on blaming Thulethu.

'What is the matter with him?' she would moan. 'Why does God punish me with the child of a careless woman?'

By this time, Lindiwe was big enough to pick the boy up. I would watch her as she carried him across the room. That baby looked much, much too big for her. In size, this child looked much older than just one year.

A day later, I asked Lindiwe to feed the baby as he had not been eating properly. I don't know why, but this child had terrible trouble swallowing his food. So Lindiwe carefully spooned some *amasi* into his mouth. All the time he was crying. As he was wailing, I took that child and looked at him closely, noticing that something was very wrong with his mouth. I called over Jongile's youngest nephew and looked into his mouth, trying to see what was wrong with Thulethu's child. And then I saw.

This baby had no tonsils.

My heart went out to that little boy. Of course he had problems eating! Suddenly it all made sense, why he could not sit or crawl or do any of the things that little children do, why his eyes bulged to one side. This child was *isidalwa*. A backward child. A retarded child.

I took the baby and held him closely for a while, wishing to comfort and love him with all my heart. I then tried to make him sit up by putting him inside a cardboard box that I had padded with cushions. But it did not help.

That little boy did not live long. He died soon after the day I held him, after my in-laws had taken him to the hospital in Queenstown. God did not grant this innocent child a long, or even a happy, life. It was very sad.

So Jongile's child with Thulethu was dead. I wondered if she knew.

13

The time I had enough of my husband's affairs

I tried very hard to keep my marriage and family together, but one thing I couldn't bear was to share my husband with another woman. Girlfriends were going in and out of my husband's life all the time, and no one seemed to understand why I didn't like it. My mother-in-law was never on my side. And Nokhaya, Jongile's sister, well, she was friends with a lot of those girl-friends, so there was no support from her.

There was one time, however, that Ma tried to help me. It was already 1965, some time after Thulethu had run away to Johannesburg. I think that Ma was starting to get tired of all these girlfriends who saw her son as a man to provide for them.

'Nowam,' she said to me one day. 'Your husband has found himself yet another girlfriend. I have seen her. She is working as a domestic at a place close to Queenstown train station. Now listen to me, I am going to give you some advice. You must meet this new woman. Her name is Maggie and she is respectable and very strong. She is the one who can stand up and fight those other woman that are after your husband.'

I didn't like this advice at all. 'No, Ma,' I told her. 'I don't want to talk to any of my husband's girlfriends. I am not going to let any one of them steal my husband away from me.' I told her that I could take almost anything from her son, except to share him with another woman.

But Ma went on at me that I must get this woman on my side so that she could make sure that there were no other women my husband could make pregnant. So I did meet with her, and she promised she would tell me everything that was going on.

Shortly after this I got another job, as a domestic for a white lady in town. I had gone to see this lady in the morning, introducing myself as Vinah, the English name I had been given in school. I told her that I came from kuZwelitsha location in Queenstown, and that I had heard that she was looking for someone to clean for her.

She asked me if I had a Pass, which I did, and she told me to come back the following morning at eight o'clock to start work.

Lindiwe and Thokozile were still staying with Ma at this time, and Ngeduye came in each morning to look after little Bukelwa, so I was free to work. On the first morning of my new job, this white lady told me what she wanted me to do around the house. Then she showed me where I was to eat lunch.

'Listen, Vinah,' she said. 'You must sit out back when you eat your breakfast and lunch. Wash your plate and coffee mug in the sink outside and put them away in that cupboard outside the kitchen door.'

She gave me a plate made from enamel. My coffee mug was an old jam jar with a chip in it. This plate and jar made me feel so horrible, like I was something dirty that had to be kept outdoors.

I don't remember how much that woman paid me, but it was very little, even for those days. I cleaned the house for five days of the week, from eight o'clock in the morning to four in the afternoon, and I was so happy to go home after my day. At least this was not a live-in job. If it was, I do not think I would have taken it. I knew the only thing stopping Jongile from taking another woman to our room was the fact that I was there. Unfortunately, there was nothing I could do for those times that I went home to visit the older girls and my in-laws without him.

A few weeks later, I found out that I was pregnant once again. I still did not like my job so, after only a short time, I stopped working there. During those early months of my pregnancy, Jongile came home straight after work and stayed with me the whole evening, which surprised me a little. Before, he would leave again soon after coming back from work, saying he would be home soon but only showing up the next morning. I never asked him where he went, because I knew. He had spent the night with a girlfriend.

But later on, when my tummy was beginning to show, he stopped coming home to be with me. By that time, we had moved again. Our new room was in a four-roomed house of one of Jongile's relatives in the location outside Queenstown. Apart from my husband's relative, a young girl from the rural areas was renting a small bedroom in that house. She was using our door to come into the house. Her name was Nothemba.

Early one Saturday morning, when Jongile did not come home, I went to the house of my husband's cousin, MaDlamini. A few weeks before, Jongile and I had taken supper with her and her husband. MaDlamini had done her best to welcome me with open arms, cooking a delicious supper of baked chicken, stamped and cooked mealies, potatoes and cabbage. By the end of the evening we had become very good friends.

So on that Saturday morning, when it was still dark, I went to see MaDlamini. She told me that this Nothemba, the woman who was sharing the house with us, was having an affair with my husband. She said that they sometimes spent the night together at the house of one of Jongile's friends.

That was when I just couldn't bear it any longer. Something inside me snapped. I don't know. Maybe there are some who will say that it was my fault, that I should not have made such a thing about my husband having girlfriends. That I was the one making the problems. But I could not help myself.

I left MaDlamini's house and went to look for my husband. I was then eight-and-a-half months pregnant. I took a table knife along because already in those days you could get into trouble walking alone when it was still dark.

I went straight to the house of Jongile's friend. There I found them together. They had spent the night in each other's arms.

I know it was not right, but all those years of my husband treating me so badly, making me so unhappy … I just could not take it any longer. I did something that is very hard for me to think about.

I attacked Nothemba.

Never did I think that I could hurt another person. But I did. I lost myself in fury as she fought back. Then Jongile pushed me so hard that I fell out of the door and into the side of the street, making me scrape my knees on the gravel road. Without thinking, I got up, took that kitchen knife and scratched Nothemba's face with it.

When he saw what I had done, Jongile was furious. He asked me for the knife, so that he could give it to Nothemba and she could cut me, too. I didn't want to, but he grabbed it from me.

'Go on!' I shouted. 'Give it to your girlfriend so that she can cut your pregnant wife.'

But Jongile did not give Nothemba the knife. He just looked at me until Nothemba picked up her clothes and left the room. When she was gone, I turned around and walked back to our room, Jongile following me. We did not speak about what had happened.

In the years that followed, I bumped into Nothemba twice in Queenstown. Her affair with my husband had come to nothing. She had married another man, and later divorced him. She wasn't angry when she saw me, only a bit embarrassed.

I think that when she got married she started understanding what had gone through me.

But me, I had frightened myself. That violent anger was so unlike the person I thought I was, the person I wanted to be. What had happened to my dream of being a teacher or a social worker, someone who was a good example to others? What was I now? Someone feeling such anger inside.

Finally, I knew that the time had come. I had to leave Jongile.

Part 3

Yesterday was another country
1966 to 1989

'I have walked that long road to freedom. I have
tried not to falter; I have made missteps along the
way. But I have discovered the secret that after
climbing a great hill, one only finds that there are
many more hills to climb. I have taken a moment
here to rest, to steal a view of the glorious vista that
surrounds me, to look back on the distance I have
come. But I can only rest for a moment, for with
freedom come responsibilities, and I dare not
linger, for my walk is not yet ended.'

Nelson Rolihlahla Mandela
Long Walk to Freedom, 1994

1

Going to Cape Town

I asked Jongile if I could have Mama as my midwife and give birth to my new baby at her home. He agreed.

As always, Mama and I were so happy to see each other. I told her what had happened and confessed that I still had feelings for Jongile. It was so good to be able to talk to someone who was on my side. I asked her if she thought I should go to see a witchdoctor to find out why Jongile was treating me this way and sleeping with other women.

'No, my child,' she said, softly cradling my face in her hand. 'There is nothing you or I can do about this. If this marriage is not working out, the best thing you can do is to leave him and come home.'

Four weeks later, I gave birth to a son, Wandile, my beautiful baby boy. It didn't matter to me anymore what Jongile had done once Wandile was born. All that was going through my mind was that our fourth child had been conceived of love. Because underneath all of it, I still loved my husband, just like I knew that he still loved me.

But we were just not right together anymore.

Jongile came to visit us in Hukuwa a week after Wandile was born, a very happy man now that he was father to a son. He came alone, having left Bukelwa with his parents, who, he told me, were more than happy to look after our three daughters.

I think they wanted to keep Bukelwa there because they were afraid that I would never bring her back.

It was difficult for me to see Jongile so happy with Wandile. I had had a son with my husband. Something that was very important to both him and my in-laws. He was *indlalifa*, the son of *inkulu*. In our Xhosa tradition, that means that by the time Wandile was a grown man and married, he would take care of his sisters if they had any problems and look after me and my husband when we were old.

Jongile thanked Mama for being my *umzalisikazi*, my midwife, and for bringing his son safely into the world. They chatted happily together, for there was no hidden anger between them or me. Mama even told Jongile to put a few drops of the brandy that he had bought her as a present into her coffee, and she was enjoying this very much.

I told Jongile that I would be going to Somerset West the following week to visit my brother, Ntsodo. I told him that I needed to rest and think about things. The year before, when Ntsodo had come home on a holiday, he had asked Jongile's permission for me to visit him there. He said that I looked unwell and thin. My husband had agreed.

So, a week later, Jongile took me and Wandile to Queenstown station on Sunday evening, from where we caught the train to Somerset West at midnight. I had a plan to stay in the Cape for two or three months, long enough to recover from having the baby and to think about my life and my husband.

I wasn't worried about saying goodbye to Mama, my three daughters or my in-laws because I knew that I would be coming home soon. I just didn't know how things were going to work out with my husband. All I knew was that I had to get away.

After staying with Ntsodo for a few weeks in his room in Somerset West, I found a job. This way, I could earn some money so that I could bring presents and clothes for the children when I went back home.

After I was in Somerset West for about two months, I got a letter from Jongile in reply to one I had sent him earlier to tell him that Wandile and I had arrived safely. It was this letter that made me decide to stay longer.

It was not written in my husband's hand but a woman's, and it had bad *muti* in it. I knew this because Ntsodo had opened the letter by mistake and had fallen unconscious for a short while. Who knows what would have happened if I was the one who opened that letter. It was a scary moment.

It was clear to me that Jongile's new girlfriend had read my letter to my husband, and that she had been the one who wanted me not to go back. It reminded me of that conversation between Ma and Thulethu, who had wanted me dead.

So I thought, well that's fine. I will stay here a bit longer. I knew this new girlfriend would not stay for long.

Soon after I decided to stay, I got a job with a wonderful couple with two children. Mrs and Mr Geldenhuys were Afrikaans and some of the kindest people I have ever met in my life. Never was the colour of my skin a problem with them. They treated me better than Ma ever had, and even let me live with them. They knew I did not have a Pass, but they still let me work, even though this could get them into trouble.

Mrs Geldenhuys would speak to me about her hopes, and I would tell her about my husband and children back home. She had a girl of about six years and a boy when I started working for her. About a year later, she had a baby girl. I grew very close to all her children. The firstborn girl used to say to me, 'Vinah, when I get married, I will take you away from my mother and father and you will work for me. Then I will look after you when you are very old!'

After about a year, it was with pain in my heart that I decided to go back to Queenstown to try again with Jongile. I just could not stay away from home any longer, and it was getting more difficult to hide Wandile and myself without a Pass. There was also no way that I could live in Waterkloof, the location nearby, because I heard that there people would betray those who did not have a Pass so that the police would let them stay. No, it was much safer to live with my employers, where I could hide.

Mrs Geldenhuys cried when I left, but she understood that I needed to go back to my own home, and my own family.

But going home was another disappointment.

2

Looking for a place to call home

After Wandile and I arrived at Queenstown station early in the morning, I took a taxi to Jongile's room in the location, getting there when it was still dark. He was not alone.

I ignored the woman's voice coming from the bedroom and went into the kitchen to make coffee and food for Wandile. When that was done, I sat with my husband to tell him my news from my year in Somerset West. He was very happy to see Wandile, and talked with me as if there wasn't anybody else there.

A few hours later, when the sun had risen, Jongile took me in his motorcar to his parents to see my children. I was so happy to be with my three beautiful daughters again. *Lindiwe! Thokozile! Bukelwa!* I was crying. Just looking at them, seeing how they had grown and how happy they were to see me, brought tears of happiness to my eyes. We all sat together and hugged and kissed each other.

But my happiness did not last long.

'Now that she is back, I am not good enough anymore?' Ma complained. 'Don't forget who has been looking after you all this time.'

As soon as she said this, Lindiwe, Thokozile and Bukelwa let go of me and went straight to my mother-in-law to say sorry. It broke my heart.

Over the next few months, I tried to fit in with them again. The worst was that each time I asked my mother-in-law if I could take the children to Mama, their other grandmother, she'd say no. My father-in-law did not mind if we went, but Ma was the stronger.

I tried with my in-laws for a full year, but with each passing day I knew more strongly that I did not belong here. I had to go.

I know now that I made the right decision because each time I visited my husband after that I would find another woman sleeping in my bed. Even if I had stayed, I now knew this would never change.

So I went back to the Cape, this time leaving Wandile behind. Leaving my children for the second time was the hardest thing I have ever had to do. But it was the only way I could be sure that they would be safe. The Pass laws made it impossible for me to take my children with me. They stopped me from being able to share their lives as they grew up. They stopped us from being together. But I knew that I had to go so that I could send back money for my children's schooling.

Education. The thing I never had. If my daughters were ever going to be strong women, and if my son was ever going to be able to look after his family, they needed an education. I knew that Jongile was paying a lot of money to his other children and did not have that much to spend on our children's schooling. And he did not really think that education was very important. But I did. And so paying for my children's books and uniforms and teaching became the reason for my life, the reason I left.

I also knew that if I stayed and lived with my husband's affairs, it would have broken me on the inside. In the end, it would have killed me. I never hated my husband's other children, but I did not want to share my life with them and their mothers. I could not.

I could not be with my daughters and son year after year, but I tried as best as I could to visit them every December, and to give them all that I could.

Mr and Mrs Geldenhuys were happy to have me back. Even after a year away, our friendship was still there and, over time, it grew. They even suggested that I should go to night school in Langa by train after work. In those days, trains were not as dangerous as they are today. They offered to fetch me after class. But this idea did not work because of the Pass laws.

A lady who was also Xhosa told me that I should find myself a boyfriend who had a Pass to work in Somerset West. All my troubles would be over, she said, and Mrs Geldenhuys, who was always comforting me, agreed.

At the time, there *was* a man with a Pass who was after me. He was working at a garage, and he liked me very much. He was married, but, as with many men, his wife lived in Butterworth in the Transkei. He wanted a girlfriend to keep him company. And me, I wanted to forget about Jongile and have someone to talk to. It was also good that he had a Pass because he could go anywhere and would be able to get a message to my brother or my cousin if I needed help.

So I became involved with this man. Mrs Geldenhuys took me to the clinic for pills so that I would not fall pregnant. I didn't want to mix Jongile's children with anyone else's. And for a while, I was happy.

I still went home to visit my children and Mama every year. I would always go straight to my husband's room and, knowing there was another woman in my bedroom, I'd just sit and wait until morning, when Jongile took me to my children in his motorcar.

The Geldenhuyses could see how my life was limited by apartheid, and they did what they could to make things better for me. In the end, they even drove to the Pass inspectors' office in Stellenbosch to speak to an officer after someone had reported that a black woman was working in their house without a Pass.

They pleaded with these inspectors, begging them to give me a permit so that I could stay with them. But it was of no use. All they did was stamp my *dompass* and tell me that I had three days to get out of the Cape Province.

At first, Mrs Geldenhuys said that I should stay in the main house instead of in the outside room, but I was too scared. I knew that the Pass inspectors would come back looking for me. So we decided that I should go and work somewhere else for a few months. Perhaps I could then come back. But I never did. It was too dangerous. I went from job to job, never staying more than a week in one place.

3

Trouble with the Pass inspectors

One day in December 1971, I saw a notice in the *District Mail* advertising a job with an English couple, Mr and Mrs Philips. They were looking for a married couple to stay in their garden cottage. The woman was to clean their house and the husband was to have his own work.

My boyfriend, Johnson, had a car, so we went in it to the address in the notice at six o'clock that same evening. As we turned into the driveway, I saw that the Philipses' house was surrounded by many large trees. Once we were inside the gate, I saw that the garden cottage was far from the road that the Pass inspectors used to drive along. I remember thinking that the inspectors would not be able to see me from the road whenever I had to go outside to hang out the washing or clean the windows. It was perfect.

I was so desperate for a job that I decided to lie, telling these people that my boyfriend and I were married. Mr and Mrs Philips were old enough to have two grown-up sons who lived overseas. After asking Johnson and me if we were married, they asked me about my Pass.

'I don't carry a Pass, Madam,' I said. 'I only carry an identity card.'

I told her that I did not need a Pass because I was a Coloured, and that I fell under my Coloured mother because my Xhosa father and she were not married. Luckily, neither of them spoke Afrikaans, so they did not know that I could hardly speak it, only what I had learnt at school.

The Philipses then asked us if we had children. When we said no, they looked relieved. 'Our swimming pool is not fenced,' Mrs Philips explained, 'so we cannot have small children around the house. That's why our last domestic left.'

I felt very bad, lying like that, but it was the only thing I could do. Apartheid made me a liar.

I later told Mrs Geldenhuys that I had got the job, but that I'd had to lie to get it. She was on my side. 'But what will you do if the Pass inspectors find you, Vinah?' she asked.

'Then I will tell them the truth,' I told her. 'I will tell them that I lied to Mrs and Mr Philips so that they won't get into trouble.'

And find me they did. But only after I had been working for the Philipses for eight years.

It happened one afternoon when I went out to buy a few groceries from a shop in Somerset West. On the way, I noticed a van coming along Paarl Valley Road with a CL number plate. Pass inspectors!

I froze like a buck hoping not to be spotted in the trees. Those Pass inspectors, they always drove around the neighbourhood with their Stellenbosch licence plates looking for anyone without a Pass. After all this time, they were here. And I could no longer hide.

'*Hallo, vroumens!*' said the white man behind the wheel. 'Hello, lady.'

I greeted him in return, trying to keep my voice light. '*Hallo, meneer.*'

'*Wat is jou naam? Waar werk jy? Waarvandaan kom jy?*' All these questions, asking me what my name was, where I worked and where I came from. And then, '*Maar jy is mos 'n kaffer!* But you are a kaffir!'

My head started spinning as this man asked all these answers from me. Although I tried my best to stay calm, I could not. I completely forgot to take out the cigarettes I always carried in the pocket of my dress and smoke, as if I was a Coloured lady. My brother Ntsodo had told me to do that if the Pass inspectors ever stopped me, because they knew that few black women smoked. He had also told me to put curlers in my hair if I was going out. But even though his advice was good, it was a bad day for me. I did none of these things. And I was caught.

'*My naam is Mary, meneer,*' I tried. By then, my accent was better from speaking to Afrikaans friends. But I was still nervous. 'I am going to town. I don't have a job and I am walking around looking for work, sir.'

But he did not believe me. '*Jy is mos 'n kaffer!*' he repeated.

'*Nee, meneer.*' I tried again. 'No, sir, I am not a kaffir. My mother was a brown woman and my father was a Bantu, but I fall under my mother. They were never married, sir.'

'*Kom, kom,*' he told me. 'Come on. Climb in the back of the van. You are going to jail.'

I will never forget that day; that time of day, even. It was exactly three o'clock in the afternoon when I was thrown into the back of the Pass inspector's van. On the way to Stellenbosch, the inspector stopped at Johnson's garage. He allowed me to tell my boyfriend that I was being taken off to jail.

When we got to Stellenbosch, I was put in a cell. I have never been so scared in my life. Those four walls looked so tall. There was no one else in that cell when they put me in it, but no light or windows either so it felt as though everything was close to me. I had in my mind the picture of Daniel, from the bible, being thrown into a den of lions. Only, instead of lions, I was thrown into a pit of snakes. I jumped every time my dress brushed against my leg.

After I had been in that cell for a long time, I heard a key in the door. It opened and, in the second of light that the open door let through, I saw another woman being thrown into the cell. She was thrown against the wall and fell to the ground, and then it was dark again. I could smell the wine from across the room as she sat where she fell, at first crying loudly and then swearing and singing in Afrikaans. I wanted to cry, but I was too shocked to do even that. I just stayed as far away from her as I could, trying not to think about the darkness.

Thankfully, Johnson came and bailed me out early the next day. Once he paid the seventy rand fine, I was free to go. As I left, the Pass inspectors told me that if they caught me again, they would put me back in jail and then have me deported to Queenstown.

Johnson and I drove back to Somerset West. Mrs Philips was very angry that I was late for work. I can't remember what excuse I gave her. I couldn't tell her the truth, of course, because I had lied to her about being Coloured in the first place.

Even today, when I think back to that night in that dark hole, my heart feels tight and beats fast. I can't even stand to be in crowded places without feeling as though I'm back there. Those terrifying moments when I was thrown inside those walls come back to me even when I get into a crowded taxi. Then I hear the frightening sound that those big keys made when they turned the lock of that prison cell.

My one night in jail has made me respect all those people fighting for our freedom even more.

If I ever thought to bring my small children to Somerset West, the idea dried up in that single moment. I can't say how scared I was of being caught again. I started getting up very early just so that I could clean the windows before the Pass inspectors started their search. I was trapped in a complete and ugly lie, telling Mrs Philips that my boyfriend and I were married, telling Mrs Philips I was a Coloured, telling Mrs Philips that I didn't need to carry a Pass.

And now I had to lie about spending the night in jail.

I have no words for thanking those who fought against the Pass laws and, when they were gone, against apartheid. People like Robert Sobukwe, who was in prison with my cousin Rolo. Archbishop Tutu, Mr Mandela and Mr Mbeki. All those strong and brave men and women who fought for a better life for black people. They fought for us all.

The Philipses were very good to me. I was happy, and lived in their garden cottage and worked in their house for many years without any problems. Until I fell pregnant. And that brought along a whole new set of problems.

4

Siphiwe

I was 34 years old when I fell pregnant again. After having taken these pregnancy pills for so long, I thought, *Oh! I've been using these pills for such a long time I'd better clear my blood for a while.* Some of my friends had told me that if you took these pills for a couple of years you couldn't get pregnant right away. But not me. I fell pregnant in the very first month.

I knew that I couldn't raise the child. The Philipses had made it clear that they didn't want any small children around the house, and there was no way I could move to the location with a baby. The risk was too great.

I named the boy Philip, after my employers. His Xhosa name was Siphiwe, meaning 'we are given a gift'. He was such a lovely baby, but because of the Pass laws I could not keep him with me.

By that time my boyfriend, Johnson, was old enough to take his pension from work and go back to live with his wife in Butterworth. I had met his wife before I got pregnant, and I knew she was very fond of me. She knew that we had got involved because she could not come to the Cape to be with her husband because of the Pass laws. She never blamed me for that.

So when Johnson took his pension and went back to the Transkei, he took my Siphiwe and raised him in his loving home.

I was always in touch with Siphiwe's new parents. It was good to hear about how my son was growing up. But my heart ached for my baby boy.

I finally met Siphiwe again when he was thirteen years old. The last time I had seen him, he was four years old. I had been given some money by a warm-hearted lady called Mary-Ann. She was a relative of Mrs Philips and she hated to see anybody struggle, so she gave me some money for looking after her dog, Skelm.

There was no question what I was going to use it for. I sent the money to Siphiwe's parents and asked them to send him to me for a holiday. It was going to be the first time we spent any real time together. By then, the Pass laws were over, so it was safe for him to be with me. I remember it was just before Mr Mandela was released from jail.

When my son came to see me he called me his aunt. Only the next day did he learn the truth. I found it so difficult to tell him because I didn't want to hurt his feelings. At the time, my daughter Bukelwa, who was by then nearly thirty years old and a lovely lady, was visiting me for Christmas. It was she who said that he should know the truth.

So I told him.

I told Siphiwe everything. Why he was raised by Johnson and his wife and why I, his mother, could not keep him for myself. After hearing what I had to say, Siphiwe was quiet for a bit. Then he thanked me.

'It's good that you told me,' he said. His voice sounded thick, and older than his years. 'If I did not know and you died, I might not have gone to your funeral. I would have thought it was just the death of another relative, not of my mother. My *real* mother.'

His words made me cry. And even today they make me cry when I think about that moment. Because if it hadn't been for those laws, I would have been able to see my baby, my lastborn son, grow into this wonderful person. Apartheid took him away from me. Apartheid took all of my children away from me, except for those four weeks of every year, during my holiday off from work.

How lucky I was to grow up with my mother, under Mama's guidance. I was never able to give that to my children.

5

In the years since Mama's death

Mama died on 10 August 1989, and I miss her still. What is happiness for a child without a mother? I thank God that he lent me my Mama until I was this old.

It all began one day when she was carrying her three-legged black pot outside with the help of her six-year-old grandson in order to cook stamped mealies with sugar beans. She tripped and slipped to the ground, cracking her leg.

I was home on holiday at the time, so I went to see her in hospital with Nomi and Mtshini. After a few days, she said that she felt much better and that she wanted to go home. It looked as if her leg was healing, so I went back to work for the Philipses in Somerset West.

That was the last time I saw her alive.

'*Ndlela ntle mntwana wam*,' she told me when I left my home to take the bus to Queenstown. 'Good luck, my child.'

Those were always her words whenever any of us left home.

A week later, I received a telegram from Mtshini saying that Mama had died in her sleep. I went to her funeral and took joy in seeing all her children, grandchildren and great-grandchildren there, even when my heart was so sore. They all mourned her, as I did.

Mama was not a woman that can be forgotten. She always spoke words that taught us respect and the importance of knowledge and work. She showed her family how to be loyal and honest. The world became a poorer place with her death.

My husband, Jongile, well, he became ill with kidney failure and died of hypertension in 1991. He never had a chance to vote. I last saw him eight months before he passed away. We were never divorced, even though a few years before his death he came to Cape Town and married his latest girlfriend. They then moved to East London.

My children and I buried my husband in Queenstown. His new wife threatened me when I tried to take back my own furniture, which Jongile had moved to their house in East London. I didn't try again. I had no time to lay a charge and go through the courts to get my things back. So I gave up. As I have done with so many things.

As for my in-laws, well, they died before Mama. I never went to their funerals.

The last time I saw Mrs Geldenhuys was about fifteen years after I stopped working for her. They had moved to Cape Town and so it had not been easy for me to go and visit them there. But on that day she came to Somerset West and found me. We talked for a long time, and she showed me photographs of her children, now all grown. We were so happy to be in each other's company.

Mrs Geldenhuys asked me to come and visit her, but when I telephoned her some time later I was told that she had died, unexpectedly, after a short illness. Mr Geldenhuys, too, had passed away. I cried so much. I still regret not going to their funerals, but I didn't know. They were such good people.

Mr and Mrs Philips also passed. By that time, I had worked for them for twenty-four years, and all that time they were kind to me. Now, at the age of seventy-five, I am still in touch with their two sons, who have always supported me. I owe them a great deal for that.

South Africa is now free, and so am I. I am free to live where I want to, and work where I please. I can even buy land, and no one can tell me to move off it. My grandchildren can get the best education there is to become anything they want to. For making these dreams come true, I am grateful to everyone in South Africa who found it in themselves to forgive, and live in peace.

And me? Well, I am still following my morning star, and waiting for the new sun to rise.

Epilogue

Where have all those years gone? It is now more than ten years since that beautiful day in April 1994 when I went to the polling station in Somerset West to vote for Mr Mandela.

Those memories of Mama, when I was a child, are more than half a century old. Now I am an old woman, even though inside I feel that I am still that child.

I am Nomfusi. I am that child who skips and dances and sings with the birds in the trees and the chickens in the homestead. This younger part of me is there still, in the hills and fields and rivers of the place we now call the Eastern Cape.

Mama, too, is still there. She is stamping mealies and weaving mats and cooking the samp and green vegetables in that old three-legged black pot over the fire. *Mama.*

In my mind, I hear the wind whistle through the thorn trees, dancing with their branches and playing with their leaves. And at night, the morning star shines down on my home. And we are singing.

'Laphuma ikhwezi
Laphum' ikhwezi lokusa
Ikhwezi
Ntombi yezulu khanyisa
Khanyisa ntombi yezulu.

There appears the morning star
There appears the morning star
The star, the star, daughter of the sky!
Light, light, daughter of the sky!
There comes the crack of dawn,
Beautiful morning star.'

And then,

'Afrika! Afrika! Afrika!'

I never left my home. I never left my children. How can things that are so important to a person ever really be left behind? My children and their future. That became the most important thing to me. That they would never need to be dependent on another person, or answer to them, either.

Everything I did was for them. I have learnt. I have learnt to love life and also to let go of life. My brief footsteps under this African sky, those are my legacy to this land. To my children. And to my ancestors.

The place of my birth is with me all the time. The smoke of the fires, the rush of the river and the whispers of the wind through the thorn trees. I hear these sounds, I see these sights. And I am listening to that song.

Note from Fransje van Riel

I first met Nomfusi Vinah Yekani in 1998, when she was employed as a domestic worker by my parents in Somerset West, Cape Town. How little did I know then that this extraordinary woman had such a passionate tale to tell.

As I learnt more about Nomfusi's colourful early childhood and traditional adolescent past, I, as a young woman from The Netherlands, envisaged her in an Africa of old. An Africa where cultural traditions were common, and where people were enriched by an authentic love for the land.

I was not disappointed. For the more I learnt, the more I was able to see Nomfusi's world. Her home in the rolling hills of the Eastern Cape, and her family seated around cooking pots on a wood fire. I, too, was there with Mama and the young Nomfusi, fetching the wood and hearing the gurgle of the river on its never ending course.

Nomfusi's story is special in that it reflects the emotions that any person experiences in the course of his or her lifetime: hope, love, disappointment, anger and faith. But what I found extraordinary about Nomfusi is her determination in the face of adversity. Her tenacious belief in good, and in herself. Her responsibility and sensitivity.

I would have lost out on an important part of my own life had I not known her story. I feel enriched by her thoughts and dreams, and I hope that this remarkable glimpse into her fascinating past will inspire others for a long time to come.

Fransje van Riel

Knysna, 2004

Afterword from Nomfusi Yekani

My appreciation also goes out to Fransje van Riel for believing in my story, to my children for understanding that I wanted to write about my life, to Fransje's family for giving me valuable support, and to David Tyatyeka, Edward and Charlie Taylor, Edward's wife, Jenny, and all my family for being there for me.

Vinah Yekani

Somerset West, April 2004

Glossary

amasi – a traditional African drink consisting of sour milk
bhuti – older brother
doek (Afrikaans) or iqhiya (Xhosa) – woman's headscarf
igqirha – A diviner (old term used was witchdoctor)
imithwane – pumpkin-and-runner-bean-stew
isidudu – porridge
isonka samanzi – freshly steamed bread
makoti – a young bride
molo (sg) – hello
molweni (pl) – hello
mphokoqo – crumbed mealie porridge
Nkonkobe Mountains – the Winterberg range
padkos – food for a journey, provisions
pap – maize meal porridge
sisi – older sister
thwala – Xhosa tradition where a girl is taken for marriage by
    her future husband
Transkei – former homeland, now part of the Eastern Cape
province
umbhaco – traditional African dress for women
umqombothi – African beer